In 1660, after eleven years without a king since the execution of Charles II's father, the English people decided they had had enough of republicanism. Charles returned to the kingdom which in many people's eyes was rightfully his, and was received with overwhelming enthusiasm. During his reign of twenty-five years the nation faced many problems — war, plague, and continued religious conflict — and Charles himself met opposition for his tolerance of Catholics and his secret treaties with France. His personal popularity, however, and more importantly the institution of limited monarchy, survived him.

What sort of man was able to reconcile the bitterly hostile factions which had fought the Civil War? Michael Gibson looks at his early years, and shows how his experience of virtual imprisonment by the Scots Presbyterians, desperate, disguised flight from Cromwell's armies, and finally nine years of wanderings round Europe, had made him ready to do almost anything for the sake of an easy life. But there was a more positive side to his personality. He sympathized with the sufferings of ordinary people, who also wanted no more than peace and prosperity. The high spirits of his court, though displeasing to the Puritans, set the tone for what was remembered for long afterwards as an age of pleasure and gaiety.

Michael Gibson explains the politics and diplomacy of the reign in all their tortuous complexity. He describes the achievements in the arts and sciences, which blossomed under the royal patronage. Above all, with the help of copious quotations from contemporary documents and about sixty illustrations, he evokes the spirit of the age and the character of the king who personified it.

WAYLAND KINGS AND QUEENS

Charles II

Michael Gibson

WAYLAND PUBLISHERS LIMITED

More Wayland Kings and Queens

Charlemagne	Keith Ellis
Alfred the Great	Jennifer Westwood
Henry VIII	David Fletcher
Charles V	William Rayner
Elizabeth I	Alan Kendall
Mary Queen of Scots	Alan Bold
James I	David Walter
Charles I	Hugh Purcell
Louis XIV	Christopher Martin
Peter the Great	Michael Gibson
Catherine the Great	Miriam Kochan
Napoleon	Stephen Pratt
Queen Victoria	Richard Garrett
Kaiser Bill	Richard Garrett

Frontispiece The entry of Charles II into London, 1660.

Title page A late seventeenth-century popular woodcut of Charles II.

SBN 85340 435 6
Copyright © 1976 by Wayland (Publishers) Ltd,
49 Lansdowne Place, Hove, East Sussex
Printed in Great Britain by
Biddles Ltd, Guildford, Surrey

Contents

1 Early Life and Civil War

ON 29TH MAY, 1630, there was rejoicing in England. The cannon boomed out in London and delighted Englishmen all over the country lit bonfires. They were celebrating the birth of a son and heir to King Charles I and Queen Henrietta Maria of England. The baby was named Charles. Although he was sound in wind and limb, his mother had to admit "he is so ugly that I am ashamed of him." Later, Charles confirmed his mother's verdict, saying, "Odds fish, I am an ugly fellow."

Charles was an affectionate child who admired his father and respected his mother. He soon had brothers and sisters to play with. Princess Mary was born in 1631, James, Duke of York in 1633, Princess Elizabeth in 1635, Princess Anne in 1636, Henry, Duke of Gloucester in 1640 and Princess Henrietta in 1644.

Opposite page Charles II as a young boy *(right)*, with his sister Princess Mary *(left)* and his brother James, Duke of York *(centre)*.

Below The parents of Charles II: *left* his father, Charles I, and *right* his mother, Henrietta Maria.

> "My Lord, I would not have you take too much Physick for it doth all ways make me worse, and I think it will do the like with you. I ride every day, and am ready to follow any other directions from you. Make hast to return to him that loves you. Charles P."
> *Charles, Prince of Wales, to his Governor, the Earl of Newcastle.*

Charles' early years passed peacefully enough. Like most children, he was often ill and suffered from the "cures" prescribed by the court doctors. They made him drink disgusting potions of rhubarb and senna (a shrub often used as medicine) so that he suffered alternately from sickness and diarrhoea.

At the age of eight he was given a household of his own and placed in the hands of the stately Earl of Newcastle. The Earl taught his pupil to ride, dance and fence with great skill but sadly neglected his book learning. As a result, Charles lacked powers of concentration and application throughout his life. He was always quick to grasp new ideas but lacked the mental stamina to follow them through.

Although Charles was brought up as a member of the Church of England his home background was a peculiar one as his mother was an ardent Roman Catholic. In these circumstances, it is hardly surprising that Charles was never sure which religion he preferred. His father taught him that he had been chosen by God

Below The trial of the Earl of Strafford, Charles I's chief minister. This was brought about by the attacks on him by Charles' opponents in Parliament.

A, the King.
B, his chair of state.
C, the Queen.
D, Prince Charles.
E, the Earl of Arundel Lord High Steward).
F, the Lord Keeper.
G, the Marquis of Winchester.
H, the Lord High Chamberlain.
I, the Chamberlain of the King's household.
K, the Chief Justice of the King's Bench.
L, Privy Councillors.
M, the Master of the Rolls.
N, Judges and Barons of the Exchequer.

O, the Master of Chan
P, Earls.
Q, Viscounts.
R, Barons.
S, Members of the H Commons.
T, clerks.
V, Strafford.
W, the Lieutenant Tower.
X, the Plaintiffs.
Y, the deputy's Coun officers.
Z, the Countess of Aru
+, sons of peers.

to rule England and that it was his duty to pass on all his powers to his own son in due time. The Prince of Wales was soon to learn that his father's belief in the Divine Right of Kings was not shared by many of his subjects. In the meantime, his mother delighted in teaching him the polished manners for which he became justly famous.

Charles' peaceful upbringing was brought to an end by the Bishops' Wars of 1639 and 1640. His father tried to force the Scots to accept a new prayer book, but they refused and rose in revolt. Two short wars followed in which the King was disastrously defeated. When shortage of money forced Charles I to call the Long Parliament in 1640, his opponents attacked his leading ministers. Faced by the violence of the London mob, Charles I condemned his chief minister, the Earl of Strafford, to death. To the young Prince of Wales, it seemed that all his father's difficulties arose from this fatal mistake. He vowed that the mob would never make him desert his ministers.

"I do most humbly beseech your Majesty for prevention of evils which may happen by your refusal to pass this bill [of attainder]; and by this means to remove I cannot say this accursed but I confess this unfortunate thing, forth of the way towards that blessed agreement which God I trust shall ever establish between you and your subjects." *Thomas Wentworth, Earl of Strafford, to Charles I.*

Below The execution of the Earl of Strafford, 12th May, 1641.

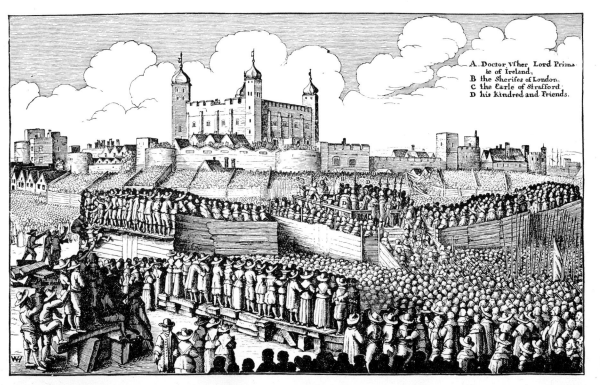

A. Doctor Vsher, Lord Primate of Ireland,
B the Sherifes of London,
C the Earle of Strafford,
D his kindred and Friends.

9

Above The raising of the Royal Standard at Nottingham in 1642.

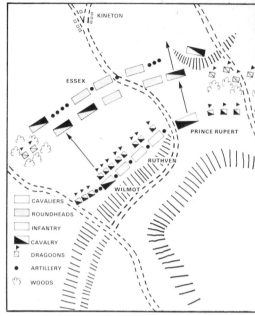

Above A plan of the Battle of Edgehill.

KINETON

ESSEX

PRINCE RUPERT

RUTHVEN

WILMOT

CAVALIERS
ROUNDHEADS
INFANTRY
CAVALRY
DRAGOONS
ARTILLERY
WOODS

Below Prince Rupert leads a charge in the Battle of Edgehill.

On reaching deadlock with the Long Parliament in 1642, Charles and the Prince of Wales marched north to York to raise an army. The Civil War had begun. The Prince of Wales was present at the opening battle of Edgehill. Indeed, he was almost captured by the Roundhead cavalry. When they attacked his position, the fiery young prince drew his pistols and urged his horse forward to meet them. Fortunately, one of his attendants seized his bridle and dragged him away to safety. This was typical of Charles. Whatever his weaknesses, he never lacked courage.

For most of the Civil War, the Prince of Wales was based at Oxford where his father had established the Cavalier headquarters. Although he accompanied his father on campaign in 1643 and 1644, he was not allowed to take part in the fighting. Then, in 1645, it seemed as if his chance had come at last—his father made him Captain-General of the West Country. In fact, this was only an empty title as all the decisions were made by an experienced general called Sir Ralph Hopton. Moreover, the Cavaliers were soon on the run.

Charles I was heavily defeated at the battle of Naseby and it was only a matter of time before he surrendered. In these circumstances, the King was anxious to move his heir to a place of safety and ordered him to seek refuge in France. This the spirited young man refused to do until he realized that his continued presence in England merely increased his father's worries.

With great reluctance, he sailed to the Scilly Isles on 2nd March, 1646. Little did he realize at that moment that he would never see his father again. The Roundheads were determined to capture the prince and sent a fleet to surround the islands. Fortunately for Charles, it was dispersed by a storm. He then set sail for Jersey and later for France. During his stay in France, he lived at his mother's court at St Germain, near Paris. Queen Henrietta Maria hoped to restore the family fortunes by marrying Charles to a rich French heiress. By this time, Charles was tall, dark and

"Lord, Thou knowest how busy I must be this day; if I forget Thee, do not Thou forget me."
Sir Jacob Astley's prayer before the battle of Edgehill.

11

Above "Jock the Scotsman" petitioning Charles I about disturbances in Scotland.

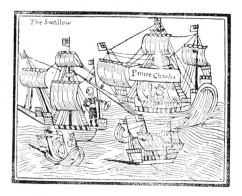

Above In 1648, as the Scots army invaded England, Prince Charles prepared his squadron to attack across the English Channel.

Right Lucy Walter, the young English girl Charles fell in love with during his stay in Holland. She bore his son, James, Duke of Monmouth, although Charles denied that they were married.

swarthily handsome. But however good looking he might be the French heiresses thought a penniless prince a poor match and remained decidedly cold.

Meanwhile, the imprisoned Charles I came to an agreement with the Scots. He promised to set up a Presbyterian Church in England for a trial period if the Scots would invade England and set him free. As a result, a Scots army invaded England in 1648 and the Prince of Wales prepared to cross the Channel. But before the arrangements could be made, Oliver Cromwell had defeated the Scots and the Second Civil War was effectively over. Nevertheless, some Roundhead warships mutinied and accepted the Prince of Wales as their commander. Full of enthusiasm, the Prince put to sea, determined to do battle with the Earl of Warwick, the Roundhead admiral. Fortunately, bad weather saved him once again from real danger. Discouraged, Charles made his way to Holland and placed the fleet in the hands of his cousin, Prince Rupert.

For the time being, Charles made Holland his base and stayed with his eldest sister Mary. She was the widow of the last *Stadtholder* (Governor) of the United

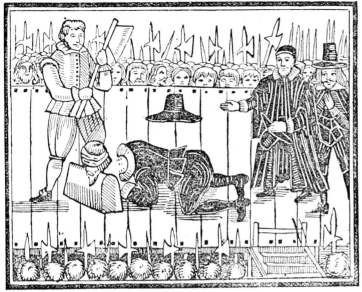

Left The execution of Charles I on 30th January, 1649. From this day for the next eleven years, England was without a king.

Provinces (now the Netherlands). During his stay in Holland he fell in love with an English girl called Lucy Walter. Many years later, people claimed that the young Prince married her at this time. This seems most unlikely and there is certainly no evidence of a marriage. However, in 1648, she gave birth to a son whom Charles recognized as his own. This baby grew up to become James, Duke of Monmouth. He was the apple of his father's eye and yet became a great embarrassment to Charles in his later years.

Meanwhile, the Prince of Wales looked for allies to help his father, but without success. Charles I was put on trial for his life and found guilty of treason. On 30th January, 1649, a bitterly cold day, the King was beheaded before a stunned crowd in front of the Banqueting Hall in Whitehall. Within a few hours, his horrified son learned that he was the exiled King of England. No one can tell how deeply Charles was affected by his father's death. At first, he must have dreamed of taking revenge upon his father's killers. But as the years went by, his hatred died away and he became convinced that the best way of avenging his father was to regain his throne.

2 Flight from the Roundheads

ON RECOVERING FROM THE SHOCK of his father's death, Charles decided to be his own master. From the beginning he refused to allow his interfering mother to rule his life or that of his brothers. When he discovered that she was trying to convert his younger brother James to Roman Catholicism, he and James left France. Shortly after this he was approached by the Scots, who offered to put him on the throne of Scotland if he became a Presbyterian. Against the advice of his leading counsellors, including Edward Hyde, he accepted these terms and set sail for Scotland.

When he reached his northern kingdom in June, 1650, he was treated with contempt by the fierce old

Right "The Scots Holding their Young Kinges Nose to ye Grinstone": a satirical engraving made when Charles travelled to Scotland to become their king.

Scots who "could find nothing but vanity and lightness in him". At first, Charles was little more than a prisoner in the hands of these "Covenanters" led by the Marquis of Argyll. But his position improved considerably when Oliver Cromwell invaded Scotland at the head of a splendid army. In September, the formidable Roundhead thrashed the Covenanters at the Battle of Dunbar. This gave Charles the opportunity he had been waiting for. The Covenanters turned to him for help and he publicly announced his conversion to Presbyterianism.

In this way, he was able to unite both the Royalist Scots and the Covenanters beneath his banner. He placed David Leslie at the head of the Scots army and for a time this skilful general held Cromwell in check. Eventually, however, the Roundheads forced the line of the River Forth and Charles had to decide whether

Above Oliver Cromwell preaches to his men before the Battle of Dunbar.

to make a dash for the English border or to retreat into the Highlands. Charles chose the first alternative, hoping that the English would rise up and join him if he appeared in their own country. This was just what Cromwell wanted him to do. The great Roundhead commander had four armies ready to pursue, round up and destroy the Scots.

At first all seemed well as Charles raced through western England. But with every mile, the Roundheads drew closer and Charles' chances of escape became more slender. On Friday 22nd August, 1651, Charles entered the walled city of Worcester and the Roundheads closed in for the kill. At two o'clock on 3rd September, the Roundhead general Fleetwood opened the battle from the tower of the cathedral. He saw the Scots opposition. Charles watched the development of the battle from the tower of the cathedral, He saw the Roundheads advancing towards the southern walls of the city and Cromwell closing in from the south-east. Realizing that his only chance of victory lay in

Below left A map showing the routes taken by Charles and Cromwell through Scotland and England in 1651.

Below right The Battle of Worcester, September 1651, showing the forces of Cromwell and Fleetwood drawn up to attack the city.

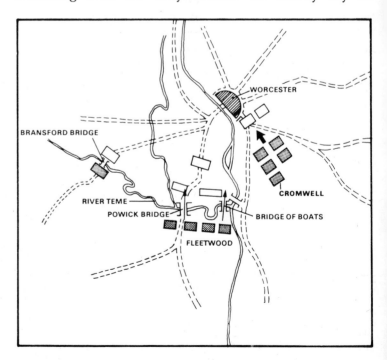

preventing the two Roundhead forces from uniting, he led the Cavalier cavalry out of the east gate and threw himself on Cromwell's forces. The Roundheads repelled his charges with the greatest difficulty. As Cromwell admitted afterwards, "it was as stiff a contest for four or five hours as ever I have seen."

Meanwhile, the Roundheads forced their way into the city and a bloody battle took place in its narrow streets. The Scots fought with desperate courage, knowing that they could expect little mercy from the Roundheads. Charles ordered the gates to be shut but in the confusion they were left open. The King stayed at his post until it was obvious that the battle had been lost. Only then did he allow himself to be led away. Once again, Charles had proved his courage in battle.

Above The thrilling escape of Charles after the Battle of Worcester. For the next six weeks he was hounded through the south of England by the Roundheads.

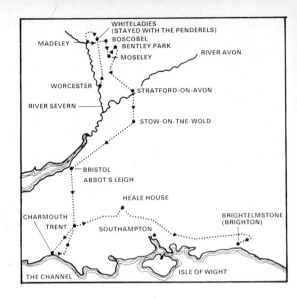

Above left The most famous story of Charles' escape from Cromwell's men tells how he hid in an oak tree while his pursuers searched below. This is a contemporary woodcut representing the King in the tree.

Above right The route taken by Charles during his flight from the Roundheads. From Brighthelmstone (now Brighton) he took a boat to France.

The next six weeks were the most exciting of Charles' life. On leaving Worcester, he hoped to make his way back to Scotland but found the way blocked by Roundhead troops. Instead, he took refuge with a family of poor woodcutters called the Penderells at White Ladies. Here his long black hair was cut short and he exchanged his fine clothes for those of a peasant before setting off across country on foot. He had not gone far before his feet were cut to ribbons by the unaccustomed exercise. He threw away his boots and walked in his stockinged feet. At Boscobel, he had his blisters seen to and rested in a hay loft. As the Roundheads were searching the surrounding woods, Charles climbed up into a huge oak tree with a supply of bread, cheese and beer and remained there warm and safe until the troops moved on. Next day, he rode off astride a great lumbering mill horse to Moseley Hall, where he was hidden in a priest's hole. From there he made his way to Bentley Park, which belonged to the Lane family.

Here, Charles changed his disguise and donned a sober grey suit and stove-pipe hat. For the next few days he made his way south, riding pillion behind Jane Lane. At Trent, Frank Wyndham met him and conducted him to Charmouth where there was supposed to be a ship waiting to take him to France.

Left Charles and Jane Lane riding through a troop of Roundheads after leaving Bentley Park.

But when they arrived, there was no ship to be seen. They decided to move on to Bridport. This was just as well, for no sooner had the King left the town than a troop of Roundhead cavalry rode in to arrest him. He had been recognized by an informer who had notified the local Roundhead headquarters.

Ignorant of how close to capture he had been, Charles made his way to Bridport. When he rode into the courtyard of the local inn, he found himself surrounded by soldiers who were staying there for the night. With great coolness, the King dismounted and pushed his way through the crowd and asked for a bed for the night. Next morning, the soldiers marched away without realizing how close they had come to capturing the most wanted man in England.

From Bridport, Charles went to Trent House where he stayed with Francis Wyndham for twelve days. Then, at last, he heard that a ship would pick him up at Shoreham, near Brighton. In the meantime, he went to Heale House five miles outside Salisbury, where he was so well hidden that even the servants did not know that they had had an extra guest for a week. When he arrived at Shoreham on 15th October, he found to his relief that the promised ship was waiting. Next day, he left England vowing to return and claim his throne.

3 Exile—and Return

WHEN CHARLES REAPPEARED IN FRANCE, people were struck by how much he had changed. His experiences had toughened him; he was quieter and more mature. At first he returned to his mother's court at the Louvre, but things did not go well. Charles hated the inactivity and the fact that he depended upon the King of France's generosity for every *sou* he spent. Then, for a moment, his hopes of regaining his throne rose when he heard that Republican England had gone to war with the Dutch.

Charles immediately offered his services to the Dutch government, but they refused them. Moreover, the Dutch were defeated and Charles saw that the Republic was stronger than ever. Then, in 1653, the Scots Highlanders seemed ready to rise in revolt. Charles prepared to join them. However, Cardinal Mazarin, who ruled France at this time, was hoping to come to an agreement with Oliver Cromwell. He made sure that the exiled king was kept so short of money that such an expedition was impossible.

Charles never forgot these years in Paris, when he was little better than a pauper. He became deeply depressed. He would have liked to go to sea to fight the Commonwealth navy or to cross over to Scotland and do battle with the Roundheads. Instead he had to while away his time in France. It is hardly surprising that he gave himself up to the pleasures of Paris—wine, women and song. To add to his misery, his mother never stopped trying to convert him to Roman Catholicism. But Charles knew that if he gave way, he would never regain his throne. Firmly but politely, he refused to take her advice.

Opposite page The swearing-in of Oliver Cromwell as Lord Protector of England, 16th December, 1653.

When Cardinal Mazarin concluded a treaty with Cromwell in October 1655, Charles was informed that he was no longer welcome in France and was given ten days to leave the country. Fortunately, his beloved sister Mary was living at Spa in Germany at this time, and offered him a home. Charles gave his creditors the slip and made his way to Spa.

Before long he was informed that a Royalist secret society called the "Sealed Knot" was planning to overthrow Cromwell. Unfortunately for Charles, Cromwell knew all about these plans thanks to his efficient secret service. When the rising took place in 1655, it was a fiasco. Only one of the leading conspirators answered the call. This was Colonel John Penruddock who captured Salisbury with a few hundred men. But when he advanced to attack Winchester, he was defeated, captured and executed. Charles blamed himself bitterly for supporting such a hare-brained venture. According to Edward Hyde, "his heart was almost broken".

Right Cardinal Mazarin, ruler of France during the 1650s.

Charles' next opportunity to return home came when Spain and England went to war in 1656. The King immediately offered his services to the Spaniards, who, after some hesitation, recognized him as King. They agreed to finance an invasion of England if Charles could find a safe landing place for his army. Alight with hope once more, Charles moved to Bruges in the Spanish Netherlands and started to recruit a mercenary army. By May 1657, he had collected 4,000 "ragged miserable creatures". But the months dragged by and the Spaniards made no move.

By the middle of 1658, Charles was more down-hearted than ever. An Anglo-French army invaded the Spanish Netherlands and defeated the Spaniards at the Battle of the Dunes. Even the death of Oliver Cromwell on 3rd September, 1658, did nothing to lift Charles' depression; Richard Cromwell succeeded his father without opposition. There seemed to be no hope for the exiled king.

Below During his exile Charles could only while away his time until he had an opportunity to return to England to claim his throne. Here he is seen dancing with his cousin Elizabeth, Princess Palatine, at The Hague.

Above Richard Cromwell, son of Oliver Cromwell, who succeeded his father in 1658. He was not able to control the Roundhead generals, however, and soon resigned.

"He is a black Monk, and I cannot see through him." *The Royalist Lord Mordaunt about General Monck.*

Then, in 1659, cracks began to appear in the structure of the Commonwealth. Richard Cromwell soon found that he could not control his ambitious generals, and resigned leaving them to their own devices. Once again, the Royalists rose in revolt, but were defeated with ridiculous ease by Major-General Lambert. The Commonwealth seemed stronger than ever. The news of this disaster reached Charles just as he was about to take ship to England. The King hid his disappointment beneath a mask of light-hearted good humour. This infuriated his friends who accused him of being hard-hearted. Did he have no feelings for those who sacrificed their lives in his service? The truth was that all his troubles had taught him to hide his real feelings.

Charles made his way to Spain where Spanish and French representatives were making peace between their two countries. The King hoped to persuade either or both governments to help him regain his throne. Cardinal Mazarin, however, the leader of the French delegation to the peace talks, thought that Charles' prospects were so poor that he refused to receive him or to consider the possibility of a marriage between the King and his twelve-year-old niece, Hortense Mancini. It seemed that Charles was doomed to failure and frustration in both private and public life.

At this moment, however, a strange, enigmatic man called George Monck entered Charles' life. General Monck had been Cromwell's man in Scotland. Following his master's death, he had watched the antics of his brother generals in England with contempt. Now he decided that the time had come for him to intervene and restore order. On 2nd January, 1660, he crossed the border into England at the head of his army. As he marched south, his enemies fell away before him. Soon he was able to occupy London without opposition.

As soon as he heard what was happening, Charles wrote to Monck. At first the suspicious general refused to read his letters. Instead, he persuaded the

Opposite page A letter from General George Monck to Parliament describing his entry into London on 9th February, 1659; the further actions of Parliament are noted below.

A LETTER

Of His Excellencie

The Lord General Monck,

To the Speaker of the Parl. From *Guild-Hall, London.*

Right Honourable,

IN obedience to the Commands received from the Council laſt night, I marched with your For-ces into the City this morning, and have ſecured all the perſons except two, ordered to be ſecu-red, which two were not to be found: The Poſts and Chaines I have given order to be taken away, but have hitherto forborn the taking down of the Gates and Portcullifes, becauſe it will in all likelihood exaſperate the City : and I have good ground of hopes from them, that they will Levy the Aſſeſs; They deſiring onely firſt to meet in Common-Council, which they intend to do to morrow morning. It ſeems probable to me, that they will yeild obedience to your Commands, and be brought to a friendly Complyance with you; for which reaſon I have ſuſpended the execution of your Com-mands touching the Gates and Portcullifes, till I know your further pleaſure therein, which I deſire I may by this Bearer ; I ſhall onely deſire, that (ſo your Commands may be anſwered with due obe-dience) ſuch tenderneſs may be uſed towards them, as may gain their affections ; They deſired the Re-ſtauration of thoſe Members of their Common-Council that are ſecured, which deſires of theirs I ſhall onely commend to your grave Conſideration, to do therein as you ſhall think moſt expedient, and, in attendance upon your further Commands, Remain

Guildhall Feb 9. 1659.

Your moſt Humble and Obedient Servant

George Monck.

To the Right Honourable William Lenthal, *Speaker
to the Parliament of the Common-Wealth of England at* Weſtminſter.

POSTSCRIPT

I ſhall become an humble ſuiter to you, That You will be pleaſed to haſten your Qualifications, that the Writs may be ſent out; I can aſſure you it will tend much to the Peace of the Country, and ſatis-fie many honeſt Men.

Thurſday Afternoon, January 9. 1659.

THis Letter from General *George Monck* from *Guild-Hall, London,* of the 9th of *February,* 1659, was read.
Reſolved, Upon the Queſtion by the Parliament, That the Anſwer to this Letter be, to ſend General *Monck* the Reſolve of the Parliament, That the Gates of the City of *London,* and the Portcullifes there-of be forthwith deſtroyed , And that he be ordered to put the ſaid Vote in Execution accordingly, and that M. *Scot* and M. *Pury* do go to General *Monck* and acquaint him with theſe Votes.

Tho. St. Nicholas, *Clerk to the Parliament.*

Thurſday, February 9. 1659.

REſolved upon the Queſtion by the Parliament, That the Gates of the City of *London,* and the Portcullifes thereof be forthwith deſtroyed, and that the Commiſſioners for the Army do take Order that the ſame be done accordingly

Tho. St.Nicholas, *Clerk to the Parliament.*

LONDON, Printed by *John Macock* in the Year 1659.

Above General George Monck,
the man who agreed with Charles
the terms of his restoration.

Republicans to hold free elections for a Convention Parliament to decide England's future. In the meantime, the General became convinced that England's one chance of peace lay in Charles' restoration to the throne, if the King could be trusted to rule legally.

On Monck's advice, Charles moved to Breda in Holland and drew up a declaration of intent. In this, he promised to call a free parliament to settle all the problems facing the country. He assured people of every religion that they would be given "liberty of conscience". He pledged himself to pay the Commonwealth soldiers their arrears in wages.

When the convention parliament met, it was full of the "King's friends". They received the Declaration of Breda with joy and unanimously invited Charles to return and take up his inheritance. The church bells were rung and bonfires were lit in towns all over Britain. The King was coming home.

Below "Roasting the Rumps in Fleet Street": a satirical engraving showing the burning of effigies of members of the Commonwealth "Rump" Parliament after the Restoration of Charles II.

4 The Restoration

ON 14TH MAY, 1660, Charles received a delegation of his faithful subjects at the Hague. Eight days later, he embarked for England on the *Naseby,* hastily renamed the *Royal Charles.* At Dover, he was greeted by General Monck "with all imaginable love and respect". On 29th May, his thirtieth birthday, he entered London to the cheers of enormous crowds. Smiling cynically, he was heard to mutter, "Had I known that I was so popular, I would not have waited so long to return."

Right Charles II boarding ship at The Hague before sailing to England, 22nd May, 1660.

Above left General Monck (kneeling) greeting Charles II at Dover.

Left The entry of Charles into London, 29th May, 1660.

"He is somewhat taller than the middle of Englishmen; so exactly formed that the most curious eye cannot find any error in his shape. His face is rather grave than severe, which is very much softened whenever he speaks; his complexion is somewhat dark but much enlightened by his eyes, which are quick and sparkling." *Sir Samuel Tuke, A Character of Charles II, 1660.*

"He was in his nature inclined
to pride and passion, and to a
humour between wrangling and
disputing, very troublesome
which good company in a short
time so much reformed and
mastered that no man was more
affable and courteous."
Clarendon on himself in Edward
Earl of Clarendon, The Life of the
Same, 1668.

Now that he was safely established in his capital,
Charles chose his leading ministers. He made Edward
Hyde Earl of Clarendon, Lord Chancellor and chief
minister. Charles would have liked to be an absolute
ruler like his young cousin, Louis XIV of France. But
as this was impossible, he put his trust in the man who
had served both his father and himself with such
loyalty. In many ways, this was a serious mistake, as
Clarendon was old and set in his ways. He expected to
control Parliament with the outworn methods of the
1640s. Even when these failed, he refused to form a
"Court Party" because he believed this would be
unconstitutional. As a result, Charles and Clarendon
gradually lost respect for each other and the King
looked to others for advice.

By tradition, the Privy Council was the King's main
advisory body. Although the King made the decisions,
he expected his Council to advise him on matters of
policy and to carry out these policies when they had
been decided. Charles' first Council, which had forty
or fifty members, was far too big to meet as a body.
Instead, Charles turned to a tiny "secret committee"
for advice. This consisted of the Earl of Southampton,
the Lord Treasurer; Sir Anthony Ashley Cooper, the
Chancellor of the Exchequer; the Earl of Ormonde;
General Monck; the two secretaries of state, Sir
Edward Nicholas and William Morrice; and the Earl
of Clarendon.

Meanwhile, Parliament was clamouring for
Cromwell's army to be disbanded. Twenty years of
military rule had created a deep fear of standing
armies in the hearts of most Englishmen. Charles was
very reluctant to agree as he wanted to retain some of
these splendid soldiers for himself. At this moment,
however, a group of extremists, called the Fifth
Monarchy Men, rose in revolt (January, 1661).
Although they were defeated with little difficulty,
Parliament's confidence had been shaken and they
agreed to Charles keeping a regiment of infantry. These
men became known as the Coldstream Guards.

Above These two contemporary woodcuts show the execution of regicides (those who killed King Charles I) after the restoration of Charles II. Charles did not want further bloodshed on his return to the throne, but Parliament and the people demanded revenge on those who had brought about his father's execution.

Although Charles did not want to re-open old wounds by punishing the men who had voted for the execution of his father, Parliament insisted on having them tried. Some twenty-eight survivors appeared in the dock of the Old Bailey. Only ten were hanged, drawn and quartered. Charles confessed, "I am weary of hanging" and pardoned the rest. To satisfy the general public's desire for revenge, Oliver Cromwell's corpse was dug up and hung from a gibbet on Tyburn Hill. For the outspoken Republican, Sir Henry Vane, however, Charles had no mercy. He was found guilty of treason and executed. "He was too dangerous to live", commented Charles wryly.

Of far greater importance was the religious problem. Once again, Charles was a model of moderation. He would have liked the various Protestant sects and the Anglican Church to unite, but this was too much to hope for after twenty years of bitter quarrelling. The new "Cavalier Parliament", elected in 1661, was full of fanatical Anglicans who were determined to punish the people who had persecuted them during the Commonwealth period. Although the King persuaded the Anglicans and Presbyterians to discuss their differences at the Savoy Conference, they were unable to come to an agreement.

Above The entry of Charles II into London before his coronation
at Westminster Abbey.

In 1662, Parliament passed an Act of Uniformity which required all parish priests to use a new prayer book. Charles tried to protect priests who refused by "dispensing" with the law; that is, he tried to place them under his personal protection. But the Speaker of the House of Commons informed the King that the House could not agree to this. Reluctantly, Charles gave way and allowed the law to take its course. In the event, two thousand priests, or about an eighth of the entire English priesthood, were expelled from their livings. The Act of Uniformity turned out to be only the first of a series of attacks on the extreme Protestants, or "Dissenters", as they were called. These acts are known as the "Clarendon Code".

Still more important from Charles' point of view was the settlement of his personal income. Parliament calculated that the King would need £1,200,000 a year to live on. In fact, this was not nearly enough, even in normal circumstances. Moreover, to make matters worse, the taxes that were made over to the King rarely brought in as much money as Parliament estimated. This meant that Charles was desperately short of money for most of his reign. The Members of Parliament were happy enough about this, as it meant that the King had to keep asking them for more subsidies. To do this he had to call Parliament frequently. Moreover, if the Members disagreed with the King's policy, they could bring great pressure to bear on him by simply refusing to vote him taxes.

Once these details were out of the way, Charles was crowned with great splendour at Westminster Abbey. Then, he chose himself a wife. Most Englishmen expected him to marry a Protestant princess, but there were not many to choose from. Most of those available were German. "I hate Germans", said the King, "or princesses from cold countries." In the end, Charles chose Catherine of Braganza, a Portuguese princess and a Catholic. According to Charles' agents, she was young and reasonably good-looking. Much more important, she had a large dowry consisting of Tangier

> "Her face is not so exact as to be called a beauty, though the eyes are excellent good, and not anything in her face that in the least degree can shock one.... Her conversation, as much as I can perceive is very good, for she hath wit enough, and a most agreeable voice." *Catherine of Braganza by Clarendon.*

in North Africa, Bombay in India and £300,000 in coin. The marriage was arranged and Catherine arrived in England in May, 1662. She made a favourable impression on Charles. "I think myself very happy", he told Clarendon.

Unfortunately, the King had already fallen under the spell of Barbara Palmer, Countess of Castlemaine, and Frances Stewart. The unfortunate Catherine had to accept these two beauties as her Maids of Honour. Although Charles always treated his wife with outward respect, he never let his marriage vows stand between him and his pleasures. The unhappy Queen was forced to turn a blind eye to his many love affairs. Moreover, to her despair, the Queen was soon to discover that she could not bear Charles the children he longed for. Some of the King's counsellors advised him to divorce Catherine and take another wife, but this Charles resolutely refused to do.

Above Catherine of Braganza, the Portuguese princess whom Charles II married in May, 1662.

Left Charles' wife Catherine had to put up with the presence at her wedding of his two favourite lovers. This is Barbara Palmer.

Right Charles' other favourite at the time of his marriage to Catherine of Braganza: Frances Stewart.

5 War, Plague and Fire

CHANCELLOR CLARENDON heartily disapproved of Charles' relations with Barbara Palmer. He openly reprimanded him for his immoral way of life. In spite of this, however, Charles and Clarendon worked quite well together for a number of years. Clarendon expected his King to superintend every aspect of government and Charles was glad to comply. No matter how long he spent drinking and whoring, the King was always up at the crack of dawn ready to head the appropriate council or committee. Charles' weakness lay not in laziness but in his inability to formulate general lines of policy. He tended to live from day to day and let the future take care of itself.

Charles and his Lord Chancellor were united in opposing the idea of a war with the United Provinces (the present-day Netherlands). The English were jealous of the success of the Dutch merchants who were trying to monopolize European trade. As a result, there was a series of clashes between the Dutch and English merchants which led to growing animosity. Even James, Duke of York was in favour of war. He was President of the new Africa Company which had been set up to exploit England's ownership of Tangier and was furious with the Dutch for interfering with his ships. Therefore, in spite of Charles' and Clarendon's personal wishes, relations between the Provinces and England grew worse until finally an English fleet attacked a Dutch convoy returning from Smyrna.

In face of this provocation, the Dutch government had no choice but to declare war on 14th January, 1665. Even then, Charles tried to negotiate a settlement before actual fighting took place. But the

> "He [*Charles*] has a strange command of himself; he can pass from business to pleasure and from pleasure to pleasure in so easy a manner that all things seem alike to him." *Bishop Burnet.*

Right It was a custom of Charles II to "lay hands" on his subjects to cure them of disease. During the Plague the danger to the King's health was too great, and he was advised to stop the practice.

Right An illustration from a plague poster of 1665 showing the burial of the dead outside the walls of the city of London.

This is to give notice, That His Majesty hath declared his positive resolution not to *heal* any more after the end of this present *April* until *Michaelmas* next : And this is published to the end that all Persons concerned may take notice thereof, and not receive a disappointment.

London, April 22.

"The people die so, that now it seems they are fain [*compelled*] to carry the dead to be buried by daylight, the nights not suffering to do it in. And my Lord Mayor commands people to be within at nine at night all, as they say, that the sick may have liberty to go abroad to take the air." *Samuel Pepys' Diary, 12th August, 1665.*

House of Commons was determined to have war and got its way. The MPs proceeded to vote Charles large sums of money, but laid down exactly how they should be spent. They did not trust their King and feared that he might use the money for his own purposes. This was the first example of what is called "Appropriation of Supply" in English history. Charles was furious at what he considered to be a blatant insult.

The 1665 Parliament had to meet at Oxford, as Bubonic Plague was raging through London. This terrible disease wiped out thousands of people and drove Charles from his capital. The Queen and Charles' mistresses were sent to Hampton Court while the King toured the West Country. In August, Charles was taken ill, but to the relief of his friends it turned out to be a mild fever and not the dreaded Plague. By September, the King was fit enough to pay a visit to Ashley Cooper's mansion in Dorset. Then, as thousands were still dying of the Plague in London, Charles spent the Christmas season at Oxford.

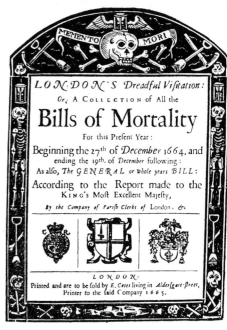

Above left Another illustration from a plague poster showing the dead being "carted off" to be buried.

Above right The title page of an official record of deaths during 1665, the year of the Plague. The page is illustrated with suitably morbid skeletons, skulls and cross-bones. The spades and pick-axes represent the digging of mass graves to bury the dead.

Left A religious fanatic, Solomon Eagle, raving to the crowd. He declared that the Plague was God's punishment to London for its evil ways.

At the beginning of 1666, the French, who were allied to the United Provinces, reluctantly declared war on England. However, the war at sea reached stalemate, as neither side wanted to risk a fight to the death. In March, Charles returned to Whitehall even though the Plague was still rampant. He took a keen interest in the running of the Navy and all seemed to be well until the Great Fire of London started on 2nd September. Soon, fanned by a strong wind, large areas of the city were ablaze. The mayor and town corporation panicked and Charles was forced to take command of the firefighting to save the rest of his capital. He ordered the houses standing in the path of the fire to be pulled down so that it had nothing to feed on. Wherever the fire was at its worst, the King and the Duke of York were to be seen directing operations.

Opposite page During the Great Fire of London in 1666 Charles II showed great courage by personally directing attempts to control the fire.

Below A scene during the Great Fire. The citizens of London are fleeing to save themselves and their belongings.

"The conflagration was so universal, and the people so astonished that from the beginning, I know not by what despondency or fate, they hardly stirr'd to quench it, so that there was nothing heard or seen but crying out and lamentation, running about like distracted creatures, without at all attempting to save even their goods; such a strange consternation there was upon them, so as it burned both in breadth and length, the Churches, Public Halls, Exchange, Hospitals, Monuments, and ornaments, leaping after a prodigious manner from house to house and street to street, at great distances one from another; for the heat with a long set of fair and warm weather had even ignited the air and prepared the materials to conceive the fire, which devour'd after an incredible manner houses, furniture and everything." *John Evelyn's Diary, 1666.*

The fire brought out all Charles' best qualities: his powers of leadership, clarity of thought and boundless energy. The King wanted to use the opportunity provided by the fire to build a new and more beautiful London on the ashes of the old medieval city. However, as so often happened during his reign, he did not have the money to make his dreams come true. All he could do was to employ Sir Christopher Wren to design a new Customs House. This fine building cost the King £10,000 of his own money. Unfortunately, it was burned down some forty years later.

Below St Paul's Church as it was before the Great Fire. The Church was completely destroyed by the Fire, and was rebuilt to a new design by Sir Christopher Wren.

Opposite page Sir Christopher Wren quickly submitted plans for the rebuilding of London after the Great Fire. *Above* is his plan for the whole city (the area destroyed by fire is shown by light shading), *below* his original model for the new St Paul's Cathedral.

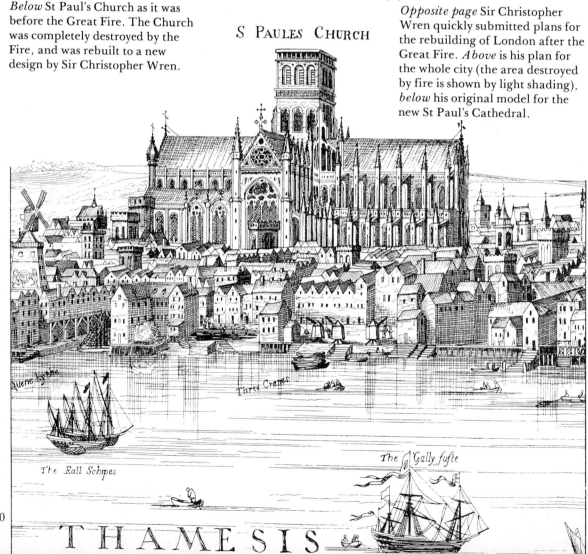

S PAULES CHURCH

Quene hythe

Three Cranes

The Eall Schipes

The Gally fufie

THAMESIS

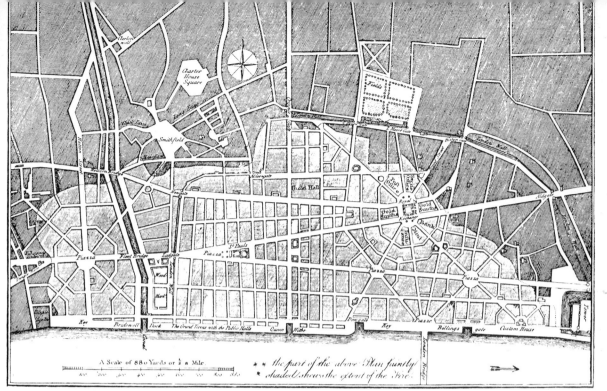

A Scale of 880 Yards or ½ a Mile

✳ ✳ the part of the above Plan faintly
✳ shaded shews the extent of the Fire.

41

Above The burning of English ships at Sheerness by the Dutch Fleet in 1667.

By 1667, Charles was desperately short of money and had to lay up many of his warships. In January, he explained his position fully to Parliament and asked for enough money to conduct the war properly. But even when the Commons voted him the money he asked for, he was little better off, as the taxes took a long time to collect. In a desperate effort to economize, Charles ordered most of his great ships to be laid up and started negotiating secretly with the Dutch in the hope that they would not attack. But the Dutch admirals saw their chance and took it. First, they attacked and captured the great fort at Sheerness. Then they broke

Above The *Royal Charles* being towed away to Holland.

through the massive chain guarding the entrance to Chatham docks, set fire to most of the warships there and towed away the *Royal Charles,* the largest ship in the English navy.

Panic spread like wildfire through the English people. They expected the Dutch to invade England at any moment. The King and his ministers were blamed for this disaster. Clarendon's London house was stoned by furious mobs. Even though Charles managed to obtain a favourable peace before Parliament met, the Commons were in an ugly mood. Someone would have to pay for the government's mistakes.

"Our people took the ship the *Royal Charles,* fitted to bear 100 pieces of cannon and with 32 guns on board. It was formerly commanded by the English Admiral Monck. Nothing more costly has been made in England, and it must have cost about 100,000 dollars in the gilding alone." *A Dutch account of the Chatham raid of 1668.*

43

The obvious scapegoat was the Earl of Clarendon. For some time, relations between Charles and his chief minister had been very strained. The old Lord Chancellor could no longer control Parliament and even opposed some of Charles' most cherished schemes, such as that for religious toleration. Obviously, the time had come for them to part company. Charles maintained, "I could not retain the Chancellor and do those things in Parliament that I desired". On 30th August, 1667, he ordered his faithful servant to hand over his seals of office. This was the signal for the Duke of Buckingham to launch a savage attack on the old man. Remembering the fate of the Earl of Strafford, Clarendon fled the country and spent the rest of his life in exile, writing his memoirs.

Charles has been bitterly criticized for his ingratitude to Clarendon. But if the cruel truth be known, the old man had long ceased to be effective, and clung to power like a limpet. If Charles allowed Buckingham to attack Clarendon, he also made sure that he could escape. He had no intention of allowing Parliament to destroy his ministers as they had in his father's day.

Right Edward Hyde, Earl of Clarendon. When Parliament demanded action after the capture of the *Royal Charles* by the Dutch in 1667, Charles sacrificed Clarendon, his Lord Chancellor, by dismissing him. In any case, relations between the two men had grown worse, and it was a relief to Charles to get Clarendon out of the way.

6 A Grand Design

CHARLES ADMIRED AND ENVIED his cousin, Louis XIV of France and wished to form an alliance with him. Most of the Privy Council and Parliament, however, opposed this because they feared the French king's growing power.

Louis intended to make France the dominant state in Europe by obtaining the largest share of the Spanish Empire on the death of his childless cousin, Carlos II. Unfortunately for Charles, Louis did not place much value on England's support following her dismal performance in the Anglo-Dutch War of 1665-67. So when Louis invaded the Spanish Netherlands (present-day Belgium) in 1667, Charles looked around for allies and formed the Triple Alliance with the Dutch and

Below The defeat of the Spanish army by the French at Bruges, in the Spanish Netherlands. This was part of Louis XIV's campaign to seize the Spanish Empire and make France the most powerful country in Europe.

Swedes. Charles hoped that the Triple Alliance would force Louis to stop fighting and also persuade him that England's support was worth having. In the meantime, he called Parliament. However, even though the MPs wanted the King to declare war on France, they were certainly not prepared to vote him the necessary money to do so.

At this time Charles told two of his closest advisers, Clifford and Arlington, that he had a "Grand Design". He was going, he said, to announce his conversion to Roman Catholicism and re-establish the religion in England, by force if necessary. For many years historians have argued about whether Charles was serious in this claim, but without coming to any firm conclusion one way or the other. Certainly, the "Design" was completely out of character with the rest of Charles' policy.

The Roman Catholics were only a small minority of his people. The last thing Charles wanted was another civil war and yet this would have been inevitable if he had followed this policy. What was the King up to at this moment? The most obvious answer is that he was trying to convince Louis XIV that he could be trusted. The French alliance had a lot to offer England. Charles hoped not only for a share in Louis' spoils of war but also the right to trade with the Spanish empire when Louis took it over.

For some months Charles conducted a series of complicated negotiations with Louis with the help of his sister Henrietta. Finally the King agreed to help Louis against the Dutch in return for a pension of £225,000 a year during the war. On the other hand, Louis promised to send over troops to England to help Charles re-establish Roman Catholicism whenever he thought the time was ripe. In May 1670, Henrietta paid a state visit to Dover and under cover of the festivities Charles signed a Secret Treaty. Shortly after her return to France, Henrietta collapsed and died. Charles was heart-broken. He had loved her deeply and sincerely.

Opposite page Charles II receiving the Duchess of Orleans at Dover before negotiating the Treaty of Dover.

S.P. Lely P.   *W. Haines S.*

The five members of the Cabal: *Opposite page: top left* John Maitland, Earl of Lauderdale; *top right* George Villiers, Duke of Buckingham; *bottom left* Anthony Ashley Cooper; *bottom right* Thomas Clifford; *this page* Henry Bennet, Earl of Arlington.

Before Charles could honour his promises to Louis he had to refit the fleet. To do this he needed taxes, so Parliament was recalled. Since Clarendon's fall, Charles had acted as his own first minister, although he showed particular favour to a group of ministers whose initials formed the word, CABAL. The favoured five were Thomas Clifford, a Treasury official; Henry Bennet, later made Earl of Arlington, the Secretary of State; George, Duke of Buckingham; Anthony Ashley Cooper, Chancellor of the Exchequer; and John Mait-Maitland, Earl of Lauderdale, Secretary of State for Scotland. These men did not form a cabinet and Charles took them into his confidence only when he had to.

Before Parliament met, Charles felt that it was necessary to deal with the rumours about his relations with Louis XIV, so he negotiated a formal alliance with France which was published and signed by all members of the Cabal. This was the same as the Secret Treaty in every way except for the clauses about Charles' conversion and Louis' promises of military help.

When Parliament met in October, Charles asked it for £800,000 to refit the fleet and announced that he was £1,300,000 in debt. It was not that Charles had been enormously extravagant. The taxes voted to him at the beginning of his reign did not yield as much as Parliament had expected, so that the King was permanently in debt. After a stiff debate, the Commons increased the King's personal income by a mere £160,000 a year and voted a further £350,000 for the armed forces. Charles was furious and vowed that he would not call Parliament again until after the Dutch War had started. To improve his financial position, the King put "a Stop on the Exchequer". That is, he stopped repaying loans to his bankers for the time being and used the money for other purposes.

Parliament, before it was prorogued (postponed), also proved an obstacle to Charles' pro-Catholic policy. Just as he was about to suspend the laws against the Roman Catholics, the Commons petitioned him to put a stop to the increase in Popery. Only by proroguing Parliament could Charles prevent it from passing a bill against the Roman Catholics. Less than a year later, Charles issued his Declaration of Indulgence suspending the laws against Dissenters and Catholics. As it was already known that James, Duke of York had become a Catholic, many people feared that Charles intended to overthrow the Anglican Church.

"We do . . . declare our will and pleasure to be, that the execution of all and all manner of penal laws in matters ecclesiastical, against whatsoever sort of Nonconformity or recusants [*religious dissenters*], be immediately suspended." *The Declaration of Indulgence, 1672.*

7 King and Parliament

IN 1672 Charles appeared to be at the height of his powers. He made Clifford a baron, Bennet an earl and Lauderdale a duke. Only Buckingham failed to receive any promotion but he was a duke already. Charles' personal life was proceeding happily. Admittedly, it was certain by this time that Queen Catherine would not be able to bear him an heir and some of his advisers were pestering him to divorce her and marry again. This he sturdily refused to do.

However, he had acquired a stunningly beautiful new mistress in Louise de Kéroualle. Louis XIV had sent her over to England, where she caught Charles' roving eye. In 1672 she bore him a son and was created Duchess of Portsmouth. Some historians have claimed that Louise acted as a spy for Louis XIV. If this is true, she was singularly unsuccessful. Her rise to favour ended the power of the insufferable Castlemaine, although Charles continued to treat her with affection and kindness.

Charles kept his word and refused to call Parliament until the Dutch War broke out. Clifford was able to raise £800,000 by normal means. James, Duke of York was made Lord High Admiral and set to work with the rest of the Navy Board to get the fleet into battle order. Then Charles deliberately provoked the Dutch into declaring war by encouraging Admiral Holmes to attack a Dutch convoy off the Isle of Wight. The combined Anglo-French fleet under the Duke of York's

Below Louise de Kéroualle, the new mistress whom Charles met in 1672.

Right The Battle of Solebay, 7th June, 1672. The English fleet lost this battle against the Dutch after the French withdrew their support.

command numbered some ninety-eight ships and was expected to sweep the Dutch from the seas. However, a Dutch fleet led by de Ruyter managed to defeat the combined navies off Southwold Bay, thanks largely to the French failure to co-operate with their allies. Charles was deeply disappointed. Moreover, the war was going badly on land where the Dutch, led by Charles' nephew, William of Orange, were putting up a spirited resistance to the French armies that were invading their country.

In 1673 Charles made Clifford Lord Treasurer and Ashley Cooper Lord Chancellor and Earl of Shaftesbury. This had the effect of dividing the King's counsellors into rival parties. Buckingham and Arlington were disappointed at failing to obtain further promotion. Moreover, Charles was so short of money that he had to call Parliament. Although the Commons were prepared to vote the King the moneys he needed, they were furious about the Declaration of Indulgence. They sent Charles an address informing him that statutes dealing with religious matters could only be suspended by Act of Parliament.

Although Charles disagreed with this interpretation of his powers, he did not want to lose the money Parliament had voted him so he pretended to consider the matter. While he was doing this, the Commons passed a bill requiring all office holders to recognize the King as head of the Church and to take the Holy Communion according to the rites of the Anglican Church. This law became known as the Test Act. It was a direct attack on the Roman Catholic members of the Government and on James, Duke of York.

In face of the Commons' determination, Charles was forced to give way on all points. He withdrew the Declaration of Indulgence, issued a proclamation against Catholic priests and Jesuits, and signed the Test Act. In return, he obtained his much-needed subsidies. But as a result of the new test, the Duke of York and Lord Clifford, as Catholics, had to resign their offices. However, Clifford was no great loss and was replaced by Sir Thomas Osborne, one of the King's ablest counsellors.

Meanwhile, the naval war went badly for the English. Prince Rupert, the new English commander,

"The truth is, as I foresaw long ago, this fleet was merely whodled out." *Rupert to Lord Arlington about his command, 1673.*

was no more successful than the Duke of York had been at getting the French sailors to play their part in the fighting. As a result, another drawn battle was fought off the Texel on 11th August. The French were openly blamed and Charles' alliance with France became more and more unpopular while the people's sympathy with the Dutch steadily increased. At this crucial moment, James Duke of York announced that he had married an Italian Princess, Mary of Modena. The Anglicans were horrified as the Princess was a Catholic and they feared that she would give birth to a son who might become a Catholic King of England. Lord Shaftesbury announced that it was the Duke's duty to divorce Mary and marry a good Protestant woman.

The Commons became uncontrollable and called on Charles to end the war. When it became clear that they would not vote him any more money, the King had no choice but to prorogue Parliament. Charles was so angry with Shaftesbury over his attack on his brother's marriage that he dismissed him from his post as Lord Chancellor. The Earl remarked savagely, "It is only laying down my gown and girding on my sword."

When Parliament met again in January 1674, the Commons were even more aggressive and attacked Charles' "evil counsellors", Lauderdale, Buckingham and Arlington. Buckingham was hounded from office and Lauderdale and Arlington only escaped dismissal by the skin of their teeth. Once again, the Commons called on Charles to end the war. In this at least he was able to satisfy them. By the Treaty of London, the Dutch agreed to dip their flags to English ships in home waters, to pay England an indemnity of £200,000 and to return all their conquests abroad.

No sooner had the treaty been signed than Charles prorogued Parliament. He had survived a severe crisis and it was obvious that he could not go on without a genuine first minister who could control the Commons. The Cabal was at an end. Fortunately, Charles had just such a man close at hand, Sir Thomas Osborne, whom he now made Earl of Danby.

8 Court and Country

IN SPITE OF HIS PEOPLE'S VIOLENT OPPOSITION to the French alliance, Charles was determined to remain on friendly terms with Louis XIV. To reduce the French King's anger at his desertion, Charles allowed him to continue recruiting mercenaries in Britain. At home, Charles decided to do without Parliament until Danby felt that he could handle the unruly Commons. So while Charles hunted at Newmarket and diverted himself with his "ladies" at Windsor, Danby re-organized the customs service, obtained new loans from the bankers and encouraged the English merchants to expand their trade while the Dutch and French were still fighting.

Below The Battle of Seneffe, fought in Belgium between the Dutch and the French on 11th August, 1674.

"I am not able to express how much his Majesty's honour and interest abroad are weakened by some proceedings of the Parliament at home, which they reckon upon, as the French in ancient times were wont to do, as a certain diversion." *William Godolphin to Arlington, 20th June, 1675.*

However, it soon became clear that Charles could not play an important part in European affairs without the money that only Parliament could supply. Danby believed that he could build up a "Court Party" by the skilful use of the royal patronage, that is, by distributing offices, lands, pensions and titles. However, this was not as easy as it might appear. He had very little money to play with and there were other people, like the foreign ambassadors, who had the same idea. Louis XIV was more than content to see Charles reduced to poverty so the French ambassador bribed MPs to vote against the government. Moreover, Danby was attacked by Charles' former ministers, Buckingham and Arlington.

With the reluctant support of the King, Danby threw himself into the task of suppressing the Presbyterians and Catholics. However, this did nothing to calm the Commons when they were recalled in April 1675. They immediately launched an attack on the hated Lauderdale and asked Charles to withdraw all English troops from the French armies fighting in the United Provinces. Moreover, they only voted him £450,000 for the Navy which was no more than one year's expenditure. In June, a disgruntled Charles prorogued Parliament, even though he was a million pounds in debt and needed another half million to complete his naval programme.

Louis XIV was anxious to stop Charles calling this anti-French Parliament again and offered the King a pension of £100,000 a year to dissolve it. Such a sum was only chicken-feed, so Charles recalled Parliament in October. During the summer, Danby had worked hard to build up his "Court Party," but even so when Parliament met, there was just as large a "Country Party" consisting of his critics and their followers. As a result, Parliament only voted a further £300,000 for the Navy and Charles decided to prorogue the Houses for fifteen months to see how he would get on without their subsidies.

1676 saw Charles and Danby following completely

different policies. Charles continued to work for closer relations with France while Danby earnestly recommended an alliance with the United Provinces. Charles had his way and signed another secret treaty with France. Although Danby refused to have anything to do with this, he remained in the King's service. In the meantime, he tried to upset the "Country Party" by closing the Coffee Houses where they met to discuss their parliamentary tactics. But there was such an outcry that he was forced to re-open them.

When Charles called Parliament in February 1677, he was faced by a serious situation. The Dutch, Spanish and French ambassadors spent money like water to persuade the MPs to support their countries' foreign policies. Moreover, Buckingham and Shaftesbury were determined to ruin Danby and bring about his dismissal so that they could get back into power. The King, however, was ready for the opposition and made a better opening speech than usual. Indeed, to his delight, the Commons voted him £600,000 for the construction of new warships.

But this happy state of affairs was too good to last, especially as Louis XIV's armies were making headway in the United Provinces. The worried Commons called on Charles to use his influence to stop the advance of the French armies. The King answered that he could do nothing until he had enough money to enlarge the army. The irritated Commons sent Charles an address asking him to ally with the United Provinces. This was a breach of the royal prerogative, so the King summoned the Commons to the Banqueting Hall at Whitehall and personally reprimanded them for their audacity.

Charles did try to arrange a peace between the French and Dutch but neither was prepared to listen to him. He returned to his old policy of asking Louis for money so that he would not have to rely on Parliament. While the two Kings were still haggling over the size of the subsidy, William of Orange paid a state visit to England. Charles met his nephew at Newmarket and discussed the international situation with him. The

"As to foreign affairs ... I am for concerting the peace with the Prince of Orange to his satisfaction and making the alliance strict with him, by which many advantages may acrue to us. ... Whereas I know none from France." *Danby to Charles, 1677.*

Below William III of Orange, Stadtholder of the United Provinces (now the Netherlands). Charles was asked by Parliament to ally with William, so that England would be stronger against the French.

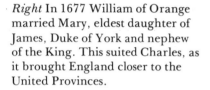

Right In 1677 William of Orange married Mary, eldest daughter of James, Duke of York and nephew of the King. This suited Charles, as it brought England closer to the United Provinces.

short, dark, asthmatic Dutchman proved a match for his shrewd uncle. During the visit, William fell in love with Princess Mary, the pretty fifteen-year-old, eldest daughter of James, Duke of York. Charles gladly agreed to their marriage, although the unhappy Mary wept for two days after hearing the news. The wedding, which took place on 4th November, was a modest affair. But when Louis XIV heard of it, he immediately cancelled Charles' subsidy!

However, when Parliament met in January 1678, Charles was able to announce that he had signed an alliance with the United Provinces and was prepared to force Louis to make peace if the Commons would vote him enough money for the army. Although the MPs voted him a million pounds, Charles did nothing, as he knew that William and Louis were near an agreement. When a peace treaty was signed, Charles asked the Commons for more money to maintain the armed forces in case the fighting restarted. But by this time, the Commons suspected the King of preparing to use force against them so they refused his request. The stage was set for a full scale show-down between King and Parliament.

9 The Popish Plot

ON 13TH AUGUST, 1678, a chemist called Christopher Kirkby stopped Charles while he was out walking in St James' Park and told him that a group of Catholics were planning to murder him. On being questioned, he admitted that a certain Dr Israel Tonge had told him about the plot. Tonge told Charles that he was going to be killed and James, Duke of York made King. Charles did not believe a word of this wild story and referred Tonge to Danby. Further questioning caused Tonge to admit that he had obtained his information from a man called Titus Oates.

This evil man seemed to know what he was talking about even though his previous career was a bad one. He had been expelled from his school, college and church living one after another for misbehaviour and had then joined the Roman Catholic Church. Somehow he had talked himself into being invited to study at an English seminary at St Omer. It was during his time at this seminary that Oates claimed that he had discovered the plot against Charles' life.

Danby did not believe Oates' lies, but saw "the Plot" as a marvellous opportunity to restore the King's waning popularity. Consequently Charles agreed to Oates and Tonge being interrogated by the Privy Council. Oates was a convincing liar and made a deep impression on the councillors. Moreover, he backed up his statements with letters which appeared to be genuine. Henry Coventry, the Secretary of State, thought that "If he be a liar, he is the greatest and adroitest I ever saw."

The next day Charles questioned Oates personally and caught him out in several lies. When Oates said he

Below A design for a playing-card of 1684. It shows Titus Oates telling Charles of the "plot" to murder him.

Dr Oates discouereth y̌ Plot to y̌ King and Councell.

Sr E.B. Godfree takeing Dr Oates his depofitions.

Coleman examin'd in New: :gate by feverall Lords.

Above Two more playing cards of 1684 showing two further stages in the investigation of the Popish Plot.

had seen Don John of Austria and that he knew of the Plot, the King asked him to describe the Archduke. Oates replied that he was tall and fair-haired, although he was actually short and dark. Oates then went on to claim that five Catholic peers, Arundel of Wardour, Powis, Petre, Stafford and Bellasis, were the chief plotters. When he told Charles that Lord Bellasis was to be the commander-in-chief of the Catholic army, Charles burst out laughing as the old man was crippled with gout.

Charles was convinced that Oates was nothing but a rogue so he went off to Newmarket as usual, leaving the Privy Council to discredit the informer. Unfortunately, Oates had some real knowledge and one of the men he accused, Edward Coleman, who had once

Above Edward Coleman being drawn to execution in 1678. Coleman was one of the victims of Titus Oates and his alleged Popish Plot.

been the Duke of York's secretary, was found to have written some incriminating letters to leading Roman Catholics abroad. Although he said nothing about murdering the King, the unfortunate man did write of the possibility of the English Roman Catholics regaining control of the country with French financial help. This was enough to convince the Privy Council that there should be a full investigation.

In the meantime, rumours of the Plot spread throughout London. Then on 12th October, it was discovered that Sir Edmund Berry Godfrey, an important magistrate, had disappeared. Five days later, his body was found in a ditch at the bottom of Primrose Hill. He had been strangled and run through with his own sword. As he had interviewed Oates and taken

"We now have a mighty work in our hands, no less than the conversion of three kingdoms and by that the utter subduing of a pestilent heresy which has so long domineered over a great part of the northern world."
Edward Coleman's Letters.

61

down some of his "evidence", it was believed that the Catholics had murdered him to keep him quiet. Charles believed that Sir Edmund, who was a very unhappy man, had committed suicide and that his body had been dressed up by Oates and his gang to look as if he had been murdered. However, to the Londoners, it seemed that this was concrete evidence that there was a plot. By the time Charles returned to London, the capital was in an uproar.

When Parliament met in October, 1678, there was little trouble as the news of the Plot had not reached many provincial areas. But it was not long before Buckingham and Shaftesbury were using the rumours to try and unseat Danby. Charles believed that Shaftesbury had deliberately manufactured the Plot, although he had no evidence of this. Both Houses of Parliament set up secret committees to investigate the matter. When Shaftesbury suggested that James, Duke of York should be removed from the Council, James voluntarily withdrew to spare his brother further embarrassment. Then the Commons passed a Test Bill excluding Roman Catholics from Parliament and sent Sir Joseph Williamson, the Secretary of State, to the Tower for giving commissions to Catholic soldiers. Charles would not allow this and ordered his release.

Encouraged by all this, Oates and another rogue called William Bedloe accused Queen Catherine of plotting against her husband. Shaftesbury and his friends hoped that this would persuade Charles to divorce Catherine and take a Protestant wife. But Charles refused to consider the idea. He might humiliate his wife by openly taking mistresses but he would not abandon her. Defeated on this issue, Shaftesbury directed his main attack at Danby. Ralph Montague, who had been dismissed from his post as English ambassador in France for misconduct, took this opportunity to take revenge on Charles and Danby. On 20th December, Montague gave the Speaker of the House of Commons a letter from Danby trying to arrange a secret treaty with France.

Below Titus Oates in the pillory. In 1683 he was fined £100,000 for accusing James, Duke of York of treason. He was unable to pay the fine, and in 1685 was pilloried, flogged, and sentenced to life imprisonment.

Opposite page The murder of Sir Edmund Berry Godfrey. This seemed to confirm that there was a Catholic plot against the King.

63

The Commons were deeply shocked by this revelation. Although Danby desperately tried to defend himself by pointing out that his accusers had also accepted bribes from the King of France, the MPs were unimpressed and drew up articles of impeachment against him. The Lords knew that Danby had always been opposed to the French alliance and had only been obeying the King's commands, so they refused to send him to the Tower.

At this point, Charles suddenly prorogued Parlia-

Right James, Duke of Monmouth, illegitimate son of Charles II and Lucy Walter. There was some support for his being heir to the throne, but Charles publicly declared that he had never been married to Lucy Walter, thus destroying his claim.

ment. It seemed to the King like 1641 all over again. He was determined not to repeat his father's mistake of allowing his chief minister to be executed. Then, without consulting his ministers he dissolved Parliament. This was a great mistake, because however awkward the Cavalier Parliament had been, it had always contained a powerful "Court Party". Now, he called a general election in a time of crisis when the majority of the voting public sympathized with his opponents.

The election was fiercely fought. There were no political parties as such in those days, but both Charles and Shaftesbury did all they could to help their supporters. The King offered posts to some candidates and prospects to others, while Shaftesbury pointed out the dangers of the situation in a flood of pamphlets. Some of Shaftesbury's supporters claimed that the Duke of Monmouth was legitimate and that he should be recognized as heir to the throne. Charles loved Monmouth deeply but he was not prepared to see James cheated out of his rights. He sent the Duke of York abroad and publicly announced that he had never been married to Lucy Walter and that the Duke of Monmouth was therefore illegitimate. In the end, the election was a resounding victory for the "Country Party" with a big majority in the new Parliament.

Faced by an angry Commons, Charles decided to steal their thunder by dismissing Danby, but first he made Danby a marquis and granted him a pension of £5,000 a year for life. The Commons were not satisfied and demanded that he be imprisoned. Charles summoned both Houses to him and announced that Danby was innocent of all their charges and that he had pardoned him for anything he might have done that was contrary to the law and would do so ten times over if necessary. Charles hoped that Danby would flee the country like Clarendon had done. But Danby was made of sterner stuff and refused to be frightened into ruining his career. Instead, he surrendered himself to Black Rod and was placed in the Tower.

"There being a false and malicious report industriously spread abroad by some, who are neither friends to me nor the Duke of Monmouth, as if I should have been either contracted or married to his mother; and though I am confident that this idle story cannot have any real effect in this age, yet I thought it my duty in relation to the true succession of the Crown, and that future ages may not have any pretence to give disturbance upon that score, or any other of this matter, to declare, that I do here declare in the presence of Almighty God that I never was married nor gave any contract to any woman whatsoever but to my wife, Queen Catherine, to whom I am now married. In witness thereof I set my hand at Whitehall 6th January, 1679." *Charles II.*

> "I have established a new Privy Council, the constant number of which shall never exceed thirty. I have made choice of such persons as are worthy and able to advise me; and am on my weighty and important affairs, next to the advice of my Great Council in Parliament (which I shall very often consult with), to be advised by my Privy Council." *Charles II, 1679.*

This was a great defeat for Charles. From the beginning of his reign, he had left the management of Parliament in the hands of his chief ministers—Clarendon, Arlington and Danby. Now, for the first time, he had to step out of the shadows and take on this difficult task himself. Charles chose some intelligent young men to help him. Robert Spencer, Earl of Sunderland, became Secretary of State, Sidney Godolphin became a Lord of the Treasury and Sir William Temple was made a Privy Councillor. The King's next move was to put the leaders of the "Country Party" where he could see them. He did this by making them all members of a new, enlarged Privy Council. His arch enemy, Shaftesbury, became the Lord President of this new body.

Right Sidney, First Earl of Godolphin, whom Charles made a Lord of the Treasury.

10 The Exclusion Crisis

IN THE MEANTIME, the Commons kept up their attack on the Duke of York. In order to satisfy the MPs, Charles proposed that certain legal limitations be placed on the powers of a Roman Catholic monarch. Such a King would have no control over ecclesiastical and judicial appointments. Most of the Council welcomed the idea except Shaftesbury, who wanted Charles to recognize Monmouth as his heir. When the King's plan was put to Parliament, it was savagely attacked by Shaftesbury's supporters, who demanded an Exclusion Bill instead. If this had been passed, it would have been impossible for a Catholic to succeed to the throne of England. When the second reading of the Bill was passed by 207 votes to 128, Charles prorogued Parliament.

Meanwhile, the Catholics were still being persecuted. On 20th June, five Jesuits were executed and shortly afterwards the Queen's physician, George Wakeman, was put on trial for his life. During the excitement, there were anti-bishop riots in Scotland and the Duke of Monmouth was sent north to deal with the rebels.

Below The Battle of Drumclog, 1st June, 1679. This was one of the battles fought by the Scottish Covenanters, who were against the system of bishops in England.

Above The Battle of Bothwell
Bridge, 22nd June, 1679. A victory
for the English under the Duke of
Monmouth against the Scots, the
battle added greatly to the Duke's
military reputation.

The Duke won an easy victory at Bothwell Bridge and
became the hero of the English Protestants. Fearing
that Shaftesbury would put Monmouth forward as an
alternative heir to the Duke of York, Charles dissolved
Parliament again. It was obvious that his attempt to
control the opposition leaders by including them in the
Privy Council had failed. He had to think of another
approach.

By this time, there were signs that the anti-Catholic
hysteria was dying down. On 18th July, Dr Wakeman
was acquitted. But before the King could cash in on
this situation, he was taken seriously ill. After a furious
game of tennis Charles went for a long walk and caught
a chill. As was the custom at the time, his doctors
purged and bled him unmercifully. His condition

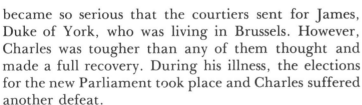

Above Two of the "chits"; *left* Lawrence Hyde and *right* the Earl of Sunderland.

became so serious that the courtiers sent for James, Duke of York, who was living in Brussels. However, Charles was tougher than any of them thought and made a full recovery. During his illness, the elections for the new Parliament took place and Charles suffered another defeat.

In face of this, Charles took a bold line. He sent both Monmouth and York out of the country, prorogued Parliament without even meeting it and dismissed Shaftesbury from his post as Lord President of the Council. Charles continued to put his trust in his young men, the Earl of Sunderland, Sidney Godolphin and Lawrence Hyde, who became first Lord of the Treasury. They became known as "the Chits" as they were only youngsters — all were under forty.

Charles' refusal to meet Parliament sharpened the divisions between himself and his critics. Shaftesbury tried to rekindle the anti-Catholic hysteria by bringing over a new group of informers from Ireland who claimed that they had evidence of a Catholic plot there. But the King was unimpressed and soon exposed the informers for the liars they were. Then Shaftesbury's supporters started to bombard the King with petitions asking him to convene Parliament. These "Petitioners" soon became known as "the Whigs". As soon as the loyal supporters of the King learned what was happening, they presented petitions "abhorring" the action of the "Petitioners". The "Abhorrers" became known as the "Tories". In this way, England's first real political parties started to emerge.

For the time being, Charles took things easily at Windsor fishing and walking in the Park until he caught another chill. On this occasion, in the absence of his doctors, he recovered quickly. However, this second illness in a year emphasized the necessity of settling the succession issue once and for all. Shaftesbury's supporters were horrified at the thought that James, Duke of York might become their King at any moment. With great daring, they persuaded the Grand Jury of Middlesex to try and charge James as a Popish recusant. Charles learned of this manoeuvre just in time and dismissed the Jury.

Charles' ministers and friends were so alarmed at the way things were going that they started to desert the King and join his opponents. The Earl of Sunderland and Sidney Godolphin suddenly found themselves able to support Exclusion and even Charles' chief mistress, the Duchess of Portsmouth, threw in her lot with her lover's enemies. By this time there was definite support for a Republican party and it was not beyond the realms of possibility that the monarchy might be overthrown. Both friend and foe alike tried hard to persuade Charles to desert his brother. But isolated though he was, Charles remained cool and loyal to James.

"There was little resort to him and he passed his day fishing or walking in the park, which indeed he naturally loved more than to be in a crowd or business." *Sir John Reresby on Charles' convalescence after his illness in 1680.*

70

In August, 1680, Charles was forced to summon Parliament, as he needed money to defend Tangier against the attacks of the wild Moors. The Commons soon showed that they cared nothing for the fate of the gallant garrison at Tangier. They were only interested in excluding James from the succession. Fortunately for Charles, they were undecided as to who should take his place. Some still favoured the Duke of Monmouth, other preferred the Duke of York's Protestant elder daughter Mary, who was married to William of Orange.

Nevertheless, the different factions united to pass the second Exclusion Bill. Charles promised to pass any legislation against the Papists they liked, but refused to allow the Commons to interfere with the principle of hereditary succession. Shaftesbury tried to frighten Charles into giving way by organizing riots in the city. But once again, Charles was determined to avoid the mistakes made by his father in similar circumstances. His reply was to bring more of his Guards into the capital.

When the Exclusion Bill was sent up to the House of Lords, Charles brought his own brand of pressure to bear. The King went to the House himself and sat or stood throughout the whole of the long debate, fixing each speaker with his steely eyes. In an atmosphere of intense excitement, the Earl of Halifax, Charles' chief adviser in the House of Lords, and the Earl of Shaftesbury fought out a battle of words. In the end the bill was defeated by 63 votes to 30. Charles could breathe again. In spite of the scaremongers, there was no revolution. The Commons had been outmanoeuvred and were at a loss for the time being to know what to do, except to ask Charles to dismiss Halifax. Charles proudly replied that "Lord Halifax was of his counsel and he did know no reason why he should not be!"

The Commons still thought that Charles would eventually give in to their demands and exclude James because of the danger of civil war. But they were wrong. In January, 1681, Charles dissolved Parliament

"Whereas James, Duke of York, is notoriously known to have been perverted from the Protestant to the Popish religion . . . if the said Duke should succeed to the imperial crown of this realm, nothing is more manifest than that a total change of religion within these kingdoms would ensue. For the prevention whereof, be it therefore enacted . . . that the said James, Duke of York, shall be and is by authority of the present parliament excluded and made for ever incapable to inherit, possess or enjoy the imperial crown of this realm."
The Exclusion Bill, November, 1680.

and dismissed Sunderland and all of the other privy councillors who had voted for the Exclusion Bill. All thoughts of an armed rising were quashed when Charles brought still more troops into the capital. Elections for a new Parliament were held and the Whigs won a large majority of the seats yet again. This time, Charles ordered Parliament to meet at Oxford. Everyone felt that England had reached a turning point in its history. Sir William Temple wrote that "the nation [is] divided into two strong factions with the greatest heats and animosities, and [is] ready to break into violence on the first occasion."

When Charles moved to Oxford, he stationed his household troops in the villages around the town. To show his confidence, he took the Queen, the Duchess of Portsmouth and Nell Gwynn with him and enjoyed a day at the Burford races. When the King opened

Below The most famous of Charles' mistresses — Nell Gwynn.

Parliament, he spoke more forcibly than usual. He told the Houses: "I, who will never use arbitrary government myself, am resolved, not to suffer it in others." He explained that though he was prepared to place limitations upon the powers of a Roman Catholic successor, he would not agree to the exclusion of his brother. The Commons decided not to debate the Exclusion issue for a week so that further negotiations could take place.

Shaftesbury told the King that the whole matter could be settled immediately if he would recognise Monmouth as his heir. This Charles said he would never do, claiming "I have law and reason and all right thinking men on my side". As a result, yet another Exclusion bill was introduced. However, on Monday, 28th March, Charles drove to the House of Lords. Once there, he changed quickly into his state robes and entered the chamber in such a hurry that his crown was lopsided. Then, without more ado, he prorogued Parliament.

Curiously, there were no demonstrations or riots. The members went back quietly to their own homes. Why was there no revolution? On the one hand, the memory of Charles I's reign was still fresh in most people's minds. No-one wanted another civil war. On the other hand, the leaders of the Opposition only saw this as another of the King's despairing manoeuvres. After all, they thought, he would have to call another Parliament again in a short time and then they would force him to do their bidding.

What gave Charles the courage to dissolve Parliament? The key seems to lie in Louis XIV's promise, given during the Oxford Parliament, that he would supply Charles with troops if there was a civil war. In addition, he offered him an immediate gift of £480,000 and payments of £120,000 a year for two years. Moreover, Charles calculated correctly that the English people were becoming bored with the Popish Plot and would not rush to arms to put the Duke of Monmouth on the throne.

> "He stood at bold defiance with his Prince,
> Held up the Buckler of the People's Cause,
> Against the Crown and skulk'd behind the Laws,
> The wish'd occasion of the Plot he takes;
> Some Circumstances finds, but more he makes."
>
> *The Royalist view of Shaftesbury as expressed by Dryden in* Absalom and Achitophel, 1681.

> "My Lords and Gentlemen, that all the world may see to what a point we are come, that we are not like to have a good end, when the divisions at the beginning are such: therefore, my Lord Chancellor, do as I have commanded you." *Charles' Dissolution of the Third Exclusion Parliament on 28th March, 1681*

11 The Royal Counter-attack

AS DAY FOLLOWED DAY without any sign of the threatened civil war breaking out, Charles' confidence grew until he felt strong enough to hit back. How did he do this? Firstly, he decided he would not call another Parliament unless war broke out on the Continent. Secondly, he vowed that he would do everything in his power to destroy the influence of the Whigs by excluding them from central and local government. During Charles' last years, only Tories were made Justices of the Peace, Deputy Lieutenants and Lord Lieutenants. One town corporation after another was forced to surrender its charter to the King who had them remodelled in such a way that they favoured the Tories. Thirdly, Charles had Shaftesbury arrested and committed to the Tower.

Before he could be brought to trial, however, the Grand Jury of Middlesex had to be convinced that he had a case to answer. When the case was heard at the Old Bailey, the courtroom was crowded with Whigs and Tories. But try as he would, the Lord Chief Justice could not persuade the Grand Jury to bring in a true bill against their old hero, Shaftesbury, so he had to be released. But by this time he was a sick man and his sixty years weighed heavily upon him.

Charles was not out of the wood yet. The European situation gave real cause for alarm. Louis XIV was extending the frontiers of France by a mixture of doubtful law and brute force. He laid claim to a whole series of territories that had once belonged to France and then sent his splendid army to occupy them. In 1681 his armies laid siege to the mighty city of Luxemburg and it seemed likely that a full scale

"A name to all succeeding ages cursed;
For close designs and crooked counsels fit,
Sagacious, bold and turbulent of wit...
In friendship false, implacable in hate,
Resolved to ruin or to rule the State."

Dryden's assessment of Shaftesbury in Absalom and Achitophel, 1681.

Opposite page A portrait of Charles II from the studio of J. M. Wright.

European war would break out. This was the last thing Charles wanted so he spent much of his time trying to persuade Louis to take a more moderate line. When the French King recalled his army in 1682, Charles claimed this as a victory for his diplomacy. In fact, this was very far from the truth. It merely suited Louis to lower the European temperature at that time.

Throughout 1682, everything continued to go Charles' way. The Continent remained quiet so that Charles was able to concentrate on strengthening his hold on the local government system. His greatest success came when he won control of London. A Tory mayor and two sheriffs were elected and the Tories obtained a small majority in the Common Council.

In 1683, the city handed over its charter. The new regulations gave Charles complete control over the choice of lord mayors and sheriffs. Moreover, during the same period, Charles built up an efficient administration. Laurence Hyde, soon to become Earl of Rochester, became Lord Treasurer; the Earl of Halifax became Lord Privy Seal; and Sir Leoline Jenkins became Secretary of State. The clever, if untrustworthy, Sunderland was restored to favour and to the other Secretaryship of State. In fact, Charles was so confident that he allowed the Duke of York to return to court.

For a time, the Whigs continued to hope for victory. Surely, they argued, Charles would have to call Parliament soon—but he did not. The Duke of Monmouth still saw himself as the Protestant heir to the throne and toured northern England hoping that the people would rise and join him. He was sadly disappointed. Instead of finding himself at the head of a large army, he was arrested for disturbing the peace and sent back to London. Although Charles saw to it that ne was allowed bail, he refused to have him back at court. To complete the unease of the Whigs, Shaftesbury suddenly fled to Holland and died there on 21st January, 1683.

However, if Charles was successful politically, he was

> "He mixed himself amongst the crowd, allowed every man to speak to him that pleased, went a-hawking in the mornings, to cock-matches in the afternoons (if there were no horse-races), and to plays in the evenings, acted in a barn by very ordinary Bartholomew Fair comedians."
> *An account of Charles' activities in 1682.*

Left John Evelyn, the diarist who recorded the social, political and artistic events of Charles II's reign.

not happy. He felt prematurely old. In spite of this, he continued to divide his time between the Duchess of Portsmouth and the vivacious Nell Gwynn. The King lavished both time and money on his mistresses. The diarist John Evelyn was astonished by the luxury that surrounded the Duchess of Portsmouth. Charles by this time was almost completely dependent upon her. While she was in France between February and July 1683, the King was lonely and unhappy.

With the new year (1683), Louis XIV renewed his attack on Luxemburg. The Spaniards became so worried about their position in the southern Netherlands that they declared war on France, asking both the Dutch and English to help them. But neither were prepared to do so. As a result, the garrison of Luxemburg was forced to surrender in the spring of 1684 and Spain had to sue for peace. Charles played no part in all this. Louis had long since decided that the English King was in no position to affect European affairs.

"The King sitting and toying with his concubines, Portsmouth, Cleveland and Mazarin, etc; a French boy singing love songs in that glorious gallery [*at Whitehall*], whilst about twenty of the great courtiers and other dissolute persons were at basset [*a card game*] round a large table, a bank of at least £2,000 in gold before them." *John Evelyn's Diary, 1685.*

Right Josiah Keeling, who discovered the Rye House Plot to murder the King and his brother the Duke of York.

At home, rumours reached the King's ears of a new plot to murder him. An informer, called Josiah Keeling, announced that a group of old Cromwellians had planned to murder Charles and the Duke of York as they drove past Rye House on their way back from Newmarket to London. Fortunately, the royal brothers had been forced to return earlier than expected by a fire in Newmarket, so they escaped unscathed. The plotters were rounded up without much difficulty and several turned King's evidence to save their lives.

Other informers claimed that a group of leading Whigs — including the Duke of Monmouth, the Earl of

1. Sheriff of London.	5. Sir F. Pemberton.	9. Baron Street.	13. Serj.t Jeffries.	17. Lord Howard.	21. Lord Rufsell.	25. Marquis of Hallifax.
2. Judge Wingham.	6. Sir W. Montague.	10. Sir W. Treby, Recorder.	14. Ward. ⎱ Lord	18. Col.l Rumsey.	22. Lord R.d Gentleman.	26. M.r Howard.
3. ——— Wilkins.	7. Judge Adams.	11. Sir R. Sawyer, Att.y Gen.l	15. Holt. ⎰ Rufsell's	19. Shepherd.	23. Lord Cavendish.	27. Rev.d D.r Tillotson.
4. ——— Levinge.	8. ——— Jones.	12. Sir H. Finch, Sol.r Gen.l	16. Pollexfen Counsel.	20. Lady Rufsell.	24. Duke of Somerset.	28. Rev.d D.r Burnett.
						29. Serj.t of the Tower.

Essex, Lord Russell, Lord Howard of Escrick, Algernon Sidney and John Hampden — were planning a rebellion. When they were arrested, Howard broke down and turned King's evidence. Russell and Sidney were condemned to death. Essex escaped execution by cutting his throat with a borrowed razor. Hampden got off lightly by paying an enormous fine. Monmouth fled abroad and remained there for the rest of his father's reign. As a result of the exposure of these two conspiracies, the Whig party was completely discredited and Charles and James regained most of their popularity with the English people.

Above The trial of Lord Russell, accused of planning a rebellion against the King. He was found guilty of treason and executed at the block.

12 Ill-health and Death

NOW CHARLES SETTLED DOWN TO ENJOY HIMSELF. He had "discovered" Winchester and decided to build a magnificent new palace there costing £40,000. During the day, he and his lady friends went hawking. At night they went to the theatre. The Marquis of Halifax tried to persuade the King to call Parliament, but Charles refused to consider the idea. He had enough money, he said, and had no intention of allowing Parliament to ruin his declining years.

Below A mid eighteenth-century view of Winchester, showing the palace in the centre background. Charles wanted to make it his permanent home, but he died before it was completed.

Indeed, he took advantage of the changed atmosphere in the country to have Danby released from the Tower where he had been confined for five years. At the same time, James was able to resume the duties, if not the title, of Lord High Admiral. Many Catholics who had been imprisoned for their part in the alleged Popish Plot were also released from prison.

There is no denying that Charles tended more and more towards absolutism as his life drew to a close. Even though the Triennial Act of 1664 had laid down that Parliament should meet at least once every three years, Charles refused to hold new elections. Fortunately for the King, English trade was booming so that he was able to live off the increased customs duties. He kept a formidable army camped outside London as a warning to the Whigs and both Scotland and Ireland were kept under close control. Charles maintained his close friendship with Louis, as he still had a sneaking fear that Monmouth or William of Orange might try to stage a rising somewhere in the British Isles. His main diplomatic success was to arrange a marriage between the Duke of York's younger daughter, Anne, and Prince George of Denmark.

At last, during the winter of 1684-85, Charles' health began to fail. He suffered so badly from gout that he was unable to go out walking and occupied himself by conducting experiments in his laboratory. Then, on Sunday 1st February, 1685, Charles slept badly and could hardly speak when he got up. When he sat down to be shaved, he suffered what his servants thought was "an apoplectic fit". Unfortunately, a doctor was present and bled him again and again. This was altogether the wrong treatment; the King was suffering from a severe kidney disease and this only made it worse. Amazingly, Charles rallied and appeared to be recovering until he had a relapse on the following Thursday. Once again, the doctors bled him unmercifully and it became clear that he was going to die.

Realizing that the end was near, Charles asked for a

Right A portrait of Charles II after Sir Peter Lely, the foremost portrait painter of his day.

Roman Catholic priest so that he could die in the faith. After a frantic search, his servants found Father Huddlestone who had helped the King to escape the Roundheads after the battle of Worcester. The old man was smuggled into the King's room through a secret door. Charles confessed his sins and received Extreme Unction. Later that evening, he showed a flash of his old bitter wit when he apologized to his relatives and courtiers for taking such a long time to die.

At midnight, Charles said goodbye to his wife. Poor Catherine fainted right away and had to be carried to her own room. Later, she sent word asking Charles to forgive her many failings. Charles sadly replied: "Alas, poor woman! She ask my pardon? I beg hers with all my heart." Then, he blessed those of his children who were present and was bled for the last time. After that he slowly sank and died at nearly noon. "He died as he lived", wrote John Drummond, "the admiration of all men for his piety, his contempt of this world and his resolution against death." His body was buried in the Chapel of Henry VII in Westminster Abbey.

13 Success or Failure?

THE TRADITIONAL WHIG VIEW of Charles as expressed by the historians Macaulay and G. M. Trevelyan is that Charles was neither a great king, nor a great man. On the other hand, Sir Arthur Bryant painted a much more favourable picture of Charles in his famous biography. Which — if either — of these two evaluations is correct?

As a man, many historians have accused him of being lazy. This is certainly not true. Charles worked hard but in his own way. He hated routine work and refused to spend hour after hour working his way through state papers, as Louis XIV did. Instead, he discussed his affairs with intelligent men and made up his mind after hearing the arguments for and against a particular policy. Unfortunately, the policies he chose were not always those of the majority of his subjects.

It has also been said that he lacked will-power. But once again, this does not fit the evidence. For throughout his reign, he withstood great pressure from Parliament without giving up any of his prerogative powers. He successfully defended his right to make foreign policy; to summon, prorogue and dissolve Parliament; and to control the armed forces.

Some historians have condemned Charles as a bad judge of character. And yet Clarendon, Arlington, Shaftesbury and Danby were first-class administrators. Of course, he made some mistakes. For example, neither the Earl of Southampton nor the Earl of Rochester made good Lord Treasurers. Charles is also condemned for his lack of loyalty to his ministers. But, with the exception of Clarendon, who was a spent force by the time he was dropped, Charles compares favourably with his father. Even under the greatest pressure, he refused to abandon Danby. He stopped the Commons impeaching him and released him from prison as soon as he could.

It has been claimed that Charles was ruled by his mistresses. Once again, this is untrue. Even Louise de Kéroualle never learned any state secrets. She and Charles' other mistresses could only obtain favours for themselves or for other people if Charles had already decided to give them. Certainly, everybody would agree that he spent far too much money on them and wasted far too much time in their company, but his policies were his own.

In many books, Charles stands condemned as a hypocrite — a secret Roman Catholic who never had the courage to openly acknowledge his faith. It is probable that Charles always leaned towards the Catholic Church and certainly he never showed any enthusiasm for the Anglican faith during his reign. On this count, Charles fell below the highest standards, although it was asking a great deal of a man of his breeding and education to give up his claim to his father's throne for the sake of what was in all probability a vague preference.

How successful was Charles? In foreign affairs, he was defeated in both his wars against the Dutch and had to give up Tangier. By his support of Louis XIV, he helped the French King to make many advances on the continent which English troops were to fight to regain at enormous cost during the reigns of William and Mary and Anne. Some historians like C. H. Hartmann have vigorously defended Charles' foreign policy. For them, the Dutch were the real commercial and naval rivals of England during Charles' reign, and not the French. Certainly, the French alliance had more to offer than many of his critics allowed. There was the chance that England would become the greatest sea-power in the world and might be given the freedom to trade with the Spanish Empire. On the other hand, it was not in our interests to have an all-powerful France dominating the continent and this was certainly one of the dangers of Charles' policy. Without doubt, his reign cannot be regarded as a success from the point of view of foreign policy.

In domestic affairs, the picture seems to be brighter. When Charles died, the Whigs had been defeated, the Tories were in control of central and local government, his finances were stable and there was every hope that the next Parliament would prove to have a Tory majority. This is true as far as it goes. But there could be no lasting improvement in the King's relations with Parliament so long as both Charles and James were determined to adopt policies which were at variance with those of the huge majority of their subjects. James' pro-Catholic policies soon undid all his brother's work and led to his own flight from England and the succession of William and Mary.

A more favourable view of Charles' financial expedients has been taken since Dr W. A. Shaw's research showed that Charles' annual revenue fell far short of the £1,200,000 promised him by Parliament at the beginning of his reign. The average yield was less than £900,000! Even if Charles had been the most economical of kings he could not have lived on the income Parliament provided him with. It was this chronic shortage of money that drove Charles to ask Louis XIV for subsidies.

Moreover, it has been shown that Charles obtained far less from Louis than was at one time thought. If all the subsidies he received from France are added together, they amount to less than one year's normal revenue! In the light of this research, Charles' failure in his wars and his desperate search for subsidies are more understandable and less reprehensible. Moreover, it diminishes the rôle of Charles' opponents especially during the great crisis of 1678-81. Their behaviour was often selfish and unpatriotic.

With this new information in mind, Charles' maintenance of the armed forces is all the more praiseworthy. On coming to the throne in 1660, Charles

> "Give me my just prerogative and I will never ask more."
> *Charles to Lord Bruce, 1684.*

> "Here lies a Great and Mighty King
> Whose Promise none relies on;
> He never said a Foolish Thing,
> Nor ever did a wise one."
> *The Earl of Rochester of Charles. To which Charles replied:* "It is very true: my sayings are my own; my doings, my ministers."

Above Samuel Pepys. Like John Evelyn, he kept a diary of the events of the day, which gives us a fascinating personal record of the life and times of Charles II's reign. His account of the Great Fire of London is particularly famous.

"Forgiving, humble, bounteous, just and kind:
His conversation, wits and parts,
His knowledge in the noblest useful arts,
Were such dead authors could not give,
But habitudes of those who live. . . ."

Charles II as portrayed by Dryden in Absalom and Achitophel, 1681.

inherited 156 ships from the Commonwealth. On his death in 1685 he left James 162 warships with a much larger total tonnage. During his reign, the pay and conditions of work of the officers and men of the Royal Navy were considerably improved. Much of this was the work of the professional members of the Navy Board, including the famous Samuel Pepys, but it was also due to the interest of Charles and James. Charles' choice of admirals was fairly successful. The Duke of York, General Monck and Prince Rupert were reasonably efficient commanders. Unfortunately, his most talented admiral, the Earl of Sandwich, disgraced himself early in the reign so that Charles was deprived of his services at the time he needed him most.

Charles' reign was one of considerable achievement in the arts, and the King contributed actively to the movement. This was the age of two of England's greatest poets, Milton and Dryden. The best Charles did for Milton—and this was no small thing, as he had been a member of the Commonwealth government—was to leave him alone in his retirement. Charles rewarded Dryden for his famous attack on Shaftesbury in *Absalom and Achitophel,* and granted him his Royal patronage.

The King created a fashion as a regular theatre-goer, helping to make the theatre more popular than it already was, and his Royal patronage also encouraged its development. In the world of music, Purcell was the first Englishman to write an opera, *Dido and Aeneas,* again with Charles' patronage. In the case of science, Charles' contribution was a result of his own interest. The great scientists of the age—Sir Isaac Newton, Robert Hooke, Robert Boyle and Sir Edmund Halley—were all members of the Royal Society, to which the King granted a Royal charter in 1662.

It is in his loyalty to his family that we see Charles at his best. He put up with his mother's interference with unfailing good humour and tact. He loved his eldest sister Mary deeply. Indeed, one of the reasons for his dislike of the Dutch was the shabby way they treated

Opposite page The Red Bull Playhouse, opened in 1660, the year of Charles' restoration.

her on the death of her husband the Stadtholder, William II. Henrietta (Minette) was his favourite sister and Charles was deeply distressed by her tragic death in 1670. Nevertheless, the most impressive evidence of his family loyalty was his treatment of his brother James. Although Charles did not like his narrow-minded, difficult brother, he stood by him throughout the Exclusion Crisis and left him a rich and powerful country.

Charles II was certainly one of the most gifted Kings to sit on the English throne, even if he was not one of the greatest or the most successful.

Right A miniature of Charles by S. Cooper.

Principal Characters

COOPER, ANTHONY ASHLEY, EARL OF SHAFTESBURY (1621-1683). Brilliant administrator, served Charles II as Chancellor of the Exchequer and Lord President of the Council. Quarrelled with Charles over foreign policy and the succession. Became the first leader of the Whigs.

BENNET, HENRY, EARL OF ARLINGTON (1618-1685). Personal friend of Charles and an able administrator. Served as Secretary of State and controlled the Commons for Charles for many years. Engineered the Triple Alliance of 1668.

CATHERINE OF BRAGANZA (1638-1705). Portuguese Princess. Married Charles in 1662. Brought a large dowry with her, including Bombay in India and Tangier in North Africa. Had to put up with Charles' string of mistresses but was always treated with courtesy by the King. Charles refused to divorce her when it became known that she could not bear children.

CLIFFORD, SIR THOMAS (1630-1673). Member of the so-called Cabal. Served as a Treasury commissioner. Forced out of office by the Test Act as he was a Catholic.

HYDE, EDWARD, EARL OF CLARENDON (1608-1674). Was first minister to both Charles I and Charles II. Looked after Charles II's interests during his exile and helped to bring about his restoration. Served as his first minister between 1660 and 1667. Blamed for the disasters of the Anglo-Dutch war and fled abroad in 1667 where he wrote his *History of the Great Rebellion* and an *Autobiography*.

HYDE, LAURENCE, EARL OF ROCHESTER (1641-1711). Second son of Edward Hyde, Earl of Clarendon. One of the "Chits", and became Lord Treasurer in 1679. Deserted Charles during the Exclusion Crisis. Was a High Anglican.

FITZROY, JAMES, DUKE OF MONMOUTH (1647-1685). Illegitimate son of Charles and Lucy Walter. Enthusiastic Protestant and good soldier. Defeated the Scots at Bothwell Bridge (1680) and was put forward as an alternative to James, Duke of York by the Whigs. Sent abroad by Charles. Executed in 1685 for rising in rebellion against James II.

GWYNN, NELL (1650-1687). Famous actress who became Charles' mistress. Bore him two sons.

LOUISE DE KÉROUALLE, DUCHESS OF PORTSMOUTH (1649-1734). French woman who became Charles' mistress. Supposed to be a French spy; if so, singularly ineffective. Charles came to depend upon her during his last years. Deserted Charles during the Exclusion Crisis.

MONCK, GEORGE, DUKE OF ALBEMARLE (1608-1670). Served Cromwell as the general in charge of Scotland. Seized control of England in 1660 and brought about the Convention Parliament. Was instrumental in restoring Charles. Rewarded with the Dukedom of Albemarle. Served as Captain-General and Admiral during the Second Dutch War.

MAITLAND, JOHN, DUKE OF LAUDERDALE (1616-1682). One of the most faithful of Charles' friends. Served as Secretary of State for Scotland; greatly hated.

OSBORNE, THOMAS, EARL OF DANBY (1631-1712). Lord Treasurer and chief minister for Charles between 1673 and 1678. Opposed Charles' pro-Catholic and anti-Dutch foreign policy. Brought down by the Whigs and placed in the Tower. The greatest part of his career lay in the future, under William and Mary.

PALMER, BARBARA, DUCHESS OF CLEVELAND (1640-1709). Charles' chief mistress at the beginning of his reign. Greedy and quarrelsome. Eventually replaced by Louise de Kéroualle. However, Charles continued to see her until the end of his life.

VILLIERS, GEORGE, 2ND DUKE OF BUCKINGHAM (1627-1688). Brilliantly gifted, totally immoral statesman and courtier. Close personal friend of Charles and a member of the so-called Cabal until the early 1670s. Soured by failure to obtain further promotion and moved into opposition.

STUART, JAMES, DUKE OF YORK (1633-1751). Second son of Charles I, brother of Charles II. Efficient soldier and sailor. Made an excellent Lord High Admiral until forced to resign as a Catholic by the Test Act. Father of Princesses Mary and Anne. Forced to leave the country during the Exclusion Crisis but Charles remained faithful to him. Rye House plotters attempted to assassinate him. Succeeded to the throne on Charles' death in 1685. Fled the country in 1688 and died in exile in France in 1701.

WALTER, LUCY (1630-1658). One of Charles' earliest mistresses. Bore him James Fitzroy, Duke of Monmouth. Claimed that Charles had married her but had lost the evidence.

Table of Dates

1630	Charles II born in London (29th May).
1642-49	The first Civil War: Charles I is eventually defeated and sends Charles II into exile.
1645-46	Charles II serves as Captain-General in the West Country, although Sir Ralph Hopton is really in charge.
1646	Escapes to France (July) and stays in Paris.
1648	Birth of James Fitzroy, Duke of Monmouth, Charles II's illegitimate son.
1649	Charles I is executed (31st January).
1649-53	The Republic: British Isles are ruled by the Rump parliament.
1650	Charles II joins the Covenanters in Scotland (March); Cromwell defeats the Scots at the battle of Dunbar (September).

1651	Charles marches into England and is defeated at Worcester (September) but escapes to France.
1651-54	Charles lives in poverty in France; his mother continually tries to convert him and his brother James to Roman Catholicism.
1652-54	The first Anglo-Dutch War: Charles' offer of help is rejected by the Dutch.
1658	Oliver Cromwell dies (September), and is succeeded by his son, Richard.
1660	General Monck marches south from Scotland and seizes control of Parliament; the Long Parliament is dissolved and free elections are held; Charles II issues the Declaration of Breda; the Convention Parliament asks Charles to return; Charles is restored (May).
1662	Charles marries Catherine of Braganza.
1665-67	The second Anglo-Dutch War: the Dutch admirals, Ruyter and Tromp, and the English admirals, the Duke of York and Monck, fight a series of indecisive actions.
1665-66	The Great Plague of London.
1666	The Great Fire of London (2nd-6th September).
1667	The Dutch sail up the Medway and tow away the *Royal Charles,* the largest battleship in the English navy; Clarendon is dismissed and flees the country.
1668	The Triple Alliance: England, Holland and Sweden ally against France.
1670	The Secret Treaty of Dover: Charles promises to win back England for the Roman Catholic Church; Louis XIV promises to help him with money and troops.
1672	The Declaration of Indulgence suspending the laws against the Non-conformists.
1672-74	The third Anglo-Dutch War: Charles makes war on the United Provinces in fulfilment of his treaty with France.

1673	Parliament forces Charles to cancel the Declaration of Indulgence and pass the Test Act. James, Duke of York has to resign his post of Lord High Admiral and Clifford his post of Treasurer.
1674	The Treaty of London ends the Anglo-Dutch war.
1678	Titus Oates invents the Popish Plot; Sir Edmund Berry Godfrey is murdered.
1679-81	The Exclusion Crisis: the Whigs led by Shaftesbury demand that the Catholic James, Duke of York be excluded from the succession; many favour the claims of Charles' illegitimate son, James, Duke of Monmouth.
1679	Charles prorogues and dissolves his third Parliament to prevent the passing of an Exclusion bill. The Covenanters rise in Scotland but are defeated by Monmouth at the battle of Bothwell Bridge.
1680	Parliament is summoned and the Commons pass an Exclusion bill; it is defeated in the Lords thanks to the efforts of Charles and the Marquis of Halifax.
1681	Charles dissolves his fourth Parliament and holds elections for his fifth. Charles calls his fifth Parliament to Oxford. The Whigs introduce another Exclusion bill; Charles dissolves Parliament before the bill can be passed.
1683	The Rye House Plot: a group of old Cromwellians plan to assassinate Charles and James, Duke of York; the plot fails. The "Whig Combination" of Monmouth, Essex, Russell, etc., are accused of complicity in the plot.
1685	Charles dies at Whitehall (6th February), and is buried in Westminster Abbey (17th February).

Further Reading

The best general introduction to every aspect of Charles' reign is *England in the Reign of Charles II* by D. Ogg (Oxford University Press, 1968). Simple introductions to the Stuart period can be found in *England and the Seventeenth Century* by M. Ashley (Pelican History of England, Penguin, 1970), *Struggle for the Constitution* by G. E. Aylmer (Blandford, 1963) and *The Stuarts* by J. P. Kenyon (Fontana, 1966).

The most critical assessments of Charles II are included in *History of England* by T. B. Macaulay (Everyman's Library, Dent, 1906), *England under the Stuarts* by G. M. Trevelyan (Methuen, 1966) and *The Later Stuarts* by G. N. Clark (Oxford University Press, 1956). A more favourable account is given in *King Charles II* by A. Bryant (Collins, 1960). The best analysis of the differing views on Charles II is *Charles II* by K. H. D. Hatley (Historical Association Pamphlet No. 63, 1966).

Perhaps the liveliest pictures of the period are painted by contemporaries; highly recommended are Clarendon's *History of the Rebellion and Civil Wars in England* and his *History of His Own Life, The Diary of Samuel Pepys* edited by R. C. Latham and W. Matthews (Bell, 1970) and *The Diary of John Evelyn* edited by W. Bray (Everyman's Library, Dent, 1973).

Interesting accounts of the background to and events of Charles II's reign are: *The Glorious Age of Charles II* by Helen Wodzicka (Wayland, 1973), *Plague and Fire* by Leonard Cowie (Wayland, 3rd impression, 1972) and *English Life in the Seventeenth Century* by Roger Hart (Wayland, 1970).

Index

Picture Credits

The author and publisher wish to thank the following for permission to reproduce copyright illustrations appearing on the pages numbered: Mary Evans Picture Library, 12 *bottom*, 15, 20, 22, 34, 39, 45, 47, 48 *top right and bottom right,* 51, 55, 58, 61, 62, 66, 67, 68, 69, 72, 77, 78, 79, 80; Radio Times Hulton Picture Library, *frontispiece*; The Mansell Collection, 23, 32; The National Portrait Gallery, 74; the remaining illustrations are the property of the Wayland Picture Library.

The maps on pages 10, 16 and 18 were drawn by John Walter.